D1026753

COOPERATIVE SALVATION

Cooperative Salvation

A Brethren View of Atonement

Kate Eisenbise Crell

WIPF & STOCK · Eugene, Oregon

COOPERATIVE SALVATION
A Brethren View of Atonement

Copyright © 2014 Kate Eisenbise Crell. All rights reserved. Except for brief quotations in critical publications or reviews, no part of this book may be reproduced in any manner without prior written permission from the publisher. Write: Permissions, Wipf and Stock Publishers, 199 W. 8th Ave., Suite 3, Eugene, OR 97401.

Wipf and Stock
An Imprint of Wipf and Stock Publishers
199 W. 8th Ave., Suite 3
Eugene, OR 97401

www.wipfandstock.com

ISBN 13: 978-1-62564-227-1

Manufactured in the U.S.A.

Scripture quotations are taken from the New Revised Standard Version Bible, NRSV, copyright © 1989 by the National Council of the Churches of Christ in the United States of America. Used by permission. All rights reserved.

Contents

Brethren Theology Series Preface

As the political and cultural privilege of Christianity crumbles, more theologians are seeking the perspective of traditions that prefigure a Post-Christendom perspective and offer other ways of believing. Anabaptist traditions, named for the practice of baptizing adults, have much to add to the discussion. *Passing the Privilege* contributes to these theological conversations from the perspective of one family of Anabaptist-Pietists in particular, known today as the Brethren.

At the dawn of the eighteenth century, a small group of Pietists gathered together to explore the scriptures and encourage one another to follow in the footsteps of Jesus. In the course of their reading, this group became convinced that believer's baptism, rather than the Christendom practice of baptizing infants, was the mandate of the New Testament. In baptizing themselves, they came to be known as New Baptists, a name that linked them to the sixteenth century Anabaptists. In the following years, these Anabaptist-Pietists found themselves in the company of Mennonite communities as both groups sought the protection of princes sympathetic to free religious expression. The pietist impulses of the early Brethren soon took on more Anabaptist leanings.

This series seeks to add Brethren voices to the contemporary discussions of faithfulness in Post-Christendom. Scholarship among the Brethren in the last century was decidedly historical in method. Constructive theological contributions have been few, and this series seeks to fill that gap. This series then hopes to reach two audiences. First, it aims to provide a Brethren perspective on Anabaptism to the conversations among Neo-Anabaptists. Second, it seeks to contribute a constructive theological resource for the Brethren themselves.

Passing the Privilege is named for an early practice of shared leadership among the Brethren. Before the Brethren adopted a paid model of ministry, congregations were led by a small group of elders. When the community gathered, these elders would share the preaching responsibility. One elder would comment on a particular passage of scripture and then "pass the privilege" to one of the others. By recalling this practice in the title of this series, we intend to identify two key values. First, books in this series will comment on both the scriptures and our context. In this way, *Passing the Privilege* is decidedly theological in nature. Second, the series will publish a variety of perspectives similar to the ways the early elders offered multiple perspectives. Rather than establish a theological method or perspective as the guiding frame for the series, *Passing the Privilege* is decidedly multi-voiced. Authors in this series, then, do not offer the definitive Brethren interpretation of any of the theological topics. Instead, they seek to contribute ideas to the continuing theological conversation among those in the Brethren tradition and beyond.

SERIES EDITORS:
Joshua Brockway
Kate Eisenbise Crell
Andrew Hamilton
Denise Kettering-Lane

Introduction

"What does it mean that Jesus died for my sins?" My brother asked me this innocent—and yet loaded—question one afternoon as we were walking home from class. He had come to visit me while I was attending seminary and had agreed to sit in on one of my classes that day. I don't remember what the class was or the topic for that day, but I do distinctly remember his question and my utter inability to answer him. This phrase is tossed around a lot in Christian circles, but very rarely is it ever explained. That little question ended up propelling me into graduate work to pursue a PhD in systematic and philosophical theology in the area of atonement theory. And yet, after wrestling with this question for years, I realize that the ideas that form my answer to that question (the ideas contained in this book) have been swirling around in my head since I was a child, and those ideas are strongly rooted in my Brethren identity.

When I was in the fifth grade, I had two best friends. One was Roman Catholic, and the other—let's call her Ashley—was an Evangelical Protestant. One afternoon, the three of us were sitting in Ashley's kitchen chatting with her mom, and Ashley's mom started to tell us a cautionary tale. It was about a wonderful man who had died after a long, productive, and charitable life. The man arrived at the pearly gates and approached Saint Peter, confident that he had lived a life worthy of eternal reward. He had worked for social justice, he had contributed his time and money to charities, and he had generally been a good man. Saint Peter agreed that he had indeed been a good man. But unfortunately, he didn't believe in Jesus. He hadn't accepted Jesus as his personal savior, and therefore, he was condemned to hell for all of eternity. When Ashley's mom finished this story, I was distraught. I felt so sorry for this man! Clearly the story had had its intended effect. And yet, something about the story didn't seem quite right to me. It wasn't until years later when I began studying theology, and especially Anabaptist theology, that I realized that this little story was really about the difference between orthodoxy and orthopraxy. Even at that young age, I had spent enough time in Sunday school in churches of the Brethren to know that faith isn't just about belief.

That conviction came up again many years later when I was on a seminary trip to visit several different kinds of worship services. On Friday night, we went to the Shabbat service at Oak Park Temple B'nai Abraham Zion, and on Saturday evening, we went to the Axis Service at Willow Creek Community Church. B'Nai Abraham is one of the oldest Jewish Reform congregations in Chicago, whereas Willow Creek is one of the first mega-churches in the United States. We attended Willow Creek's Axis service, which is designed specifically for twenty-somethings. One of the draws of this service seemed to be its use of media—huge screens with projected images, praise music, a professional band, a light show, etc. While each of these services was a new worship experience for me, it was the differences between them that made such a lasting impression.

On the night we visited B'Nai Abraham Zion, the rabbi was preaching a sermon in a series he had delivered on the subject of sacrifice. On this particular evening, he preached on the temple sacrifice system and discussed the ways that this concept might be useful (or not) to modern believers. He discussed the ideas of taking responsibility for one's actions rather than scapegoating others and sacrifice as penance rather than payment. While I cannot remember all the specifics of his sermon, I was struck by how the rabbi and his congregation found the whole idea of sacrifice to be problematic and struggled to understand it in terms of postmodern experience.

In contrast to the Shabbat service, the service at Willow Creek focused exclusively on the fact that Jesus' death on the cross was the ultimate sacrifice, that it was a sacrifice made for me, and that it was a wonderful event that revealed God's love for me. This unequivocal message was everywhere, particularly in the music, and almost every image projected onto the giant screen in the auditorium featured a cross. Jesus' suffering was glorified because it reveals how deeply God loves me; Jesus willingly sacrificed his life on the cross so that I would be saved from my sins and go to heaven. I cannot think of a time when I have been more uncomfortable in a worship setting. There were so many elements to this theology that I found unsettling, but the worst was the idea that I was responsible for this gruesome murder and that it somehow reveals God's love for me.

I had been wrestling with this paradoxical juxtaposition of love and violence for several years, but it was while sitting through that service that I finally rejected it. Since then, I have been struggling to understand the nature of salvation and to imagine a way that its completion does not depend on the suffering and death of an innocent victim, and I have found many, many Christians struggling with the same questions—both privately and in published academic work. But what strikes me is how few of these published voices come from my own tradition. It's almost as if Brethren have ceded this theological territory to other, more orthodox traditions. Most of the work Brethren scholars currently produce is either in the areas of history or ethics. Very little constructive Brethren theology is being written, and almost none of it is in the area of atonement theory. I believe there are three possible reasons for this dearth of constructive Brethren theology: Anabaptist and Pietist emphasis on ethics, Anabaptist hermeneutics, and Brethren suspicion of higher education.

One of the most important characteristics of both Anabaptism and radical Pietism that sets these traditions apart from mainline Protestantism is the insistence that living a life of ethical discipleship modeled on Jesus' teaching and example is an indispensable part of what it means to be a Christian. Therefore, Anabaptist and Brethren scholars have devoted much time and effort to defining the boundaries of an ethical lifestyle. One only needs to browse through the topical index of the *Church of the Brethren Annual Conference Minutes* to note that the overwhelming majority of issues debated through the centuries had to do with cultural accommodations.[1] Presumably, those accommodations were debated primarily because some within the tradition believed they undermined the Brethren commitment to an ethical lifestyle. Surely these ethical questions are rooted in specific theological (and even soteriological) beliefs, but rarely are these theological beliefs named as the reason for debating such questions about ethics. In general, it appears that most Brethren believe that our theology is not very different from other mainline Protestants; what separates us is the way we live. While our way of life is one of our defining characteristics, it is not true that there is nothing unique about Brethren theology.

---

1. See Keeney, *Church of the Brethren Annual Conference Minutes.*

A second factor that has limited constructive Brethren theology might be our Anabaptist hermeneutics. Noted Mennonite theologian John Howard Yoder believed that the tragedy of the Reformation was that the individual was given all the authority and responsibility to interpret Scripture.[2] Anabaptists had the corrective: communal discernment. No one individual can possibly understand the fullness of Scripture, so the process of biblical interpretation must take place within the believing community. The fact that the church functions as a hermeneutical community is the natural consequence of the Anabaptist belief in the radical priesthood of all believers (i.e., that every member is baptized into Christian ministry). The whole church should search and interpret Scripture because it is safer for the whole church to read the whole body of Scripture than to trust only the interpretations of those who are learned.[3] While there is much that is commendable about this viewpoint (it highlights the necessity of the community, it values all equally, and does not privilege some over others), it may have stymied the efforts of the few learned Brethren scholars who sought to offer their own individual views on a particular topic.

Finally, the Brethren have not always valued higher education and scholastic pursuits. The 1853 *Church of the Brethren Annual Conference Minutes* provide a clear example of this phenomenon in declaring that colleges were a "very unsafe place for a simple follower of Christ inasmuch as they are calculated to lead us astray from the faith and obedience to the gospel."[4] The implication seemed to be that formal study would somehow dilute one's faith, and thus scholarly pursuits—especially in the area of constructive theology—were not prized by the church.

Some of these views are beginning to change. For example, attitudes toward higher education are becoming more favorable.[5] But others are

---

2. Yoder, *Preface to Theology*, 339.

3. Ibid., *Politics of Jesus*, xi. Yoder notes that this is different from the Catholic notion of the teaching authority of the church because its safeguard lies in the due process in the congregation rather than the sacramental authority of the bishops (Yoder, *Preface to Theology*, 339). Jim Reimer argues that the entirety of Yoder's *Politics of Jesus* is a polemic against individualistic, existentialist, spiritualist biblical interpretation (Reimer, *Mennonites and Classical Theology*, 169).

4. Church of the Brethren, *Minutes*, 174.

5. For more on the Brethren views of higher education, see Bowman, *Portrait of a People*, 124. Bowman drew his data for this portrait from a survey called the "Church Member Profile," which sampled 1,826 Church of the Brethren members across the country about their beliefs, attitudes, and behaviors. While the "Church Member

deep-seated in the Brethren identity. Perhaps one of the reasons why the denomination as a whole is loath to split is because of our commitment to the Anabaptist emphasis on community and communal hermeneutics. Whatever the reasons, the fact remains that few Brethren theologians have emerged.[6] As a result, many Brethren folks rely on the constructive theologies written by Mennonites and other Anabaptists.

This book attempts to add a Brethren voice to the conversation on atonement, but first it offers readers some background. Chapter 1 defines the problem of atonement and provides a very brief sketch of Brethren history and theology, noting how Anabaptist and radical Pietist theology influenced one another within the early Church of the Brethren. Chapter 2 traces the historical development of many different metaphors and full-blown theories of atonement from the early church through the Middle Ages, while also pointing out some important critiques of those theories. In chapter 3, we turn to more contemporary twentieth-century models of atonement put forth by authors from a variety of Christian traditions, while chapter 4 examines the models proposed by twentieth- and twenty-first-century Anabaptist theologians. Finally, chapter 5 builds on the models from previous chapters and incorporates critiques of those models to propose a new, particularly Brethren way to view atonement specifically and salvation in general.

It is my hope that somewhere in this book, my brother will find the answer to the question he asked me so many years ago. For that reason, this book is dedicated to my brother, Jesse Eisenbise. Whether or not my answer still matters to him, I hope that it will contribute a distinctly Brethren voice to the ongoing conversation about the atonement and its meaning.

Profile" did not specifically ask members about their attitude toward higher education, the fact that the majority of sample members had some education beyond high school and that many had more post-secondary education than their parents did suggests that the predominant Brethren view of higher education is changing.

6. Of course this is not to say that there have never been any Brethren constructive theologians! There have been a handful of well-known and well-regarded Brethren theologians in the past few decades, among them Nadine Pence and Dale W. Brown, to name just a notable few.

CHAPTER 1

Atonement and Brethren Theology

"Once, when Jesus was praying alone, with only the disciples near him, he asked them, 'Who do the crowds say that I am?' They answered, 'John the Baptist; but others, Elijah; and still others, that one of the ancient prophets has arisen.' He said to them, 'But who do you say that I am?' Peter answered, 'The Messiah of God.'"

—LUKE 9:18-20

What does it mean that Jesus is the Messiah? And if he was the specially chosen son of God, why did he die—and why did he die such a brutal and humiliating death? The first Christians were sure that they had experienced something very special, and perhaps even something of God in the person of Jesus, yet he was executed by the state as a criminal. From that moment on, theologians have been trying to explain this tension, and most of their explanations have had something to do with salvation—suggesting that somehow Jesus' death on the cross achieves salvation for humanity.

However, not all theologians went along with this explanation, among them Hermann S. Reimarus. Reimaus was an eighteenth-century German theologian who completely rejected the linking of Jesus' execution and human salvation. In a secret manuscript that was only published after his death, Reimarus argued that what the apostles wrote about Jesus (which eventually developed into popular Christian doctrine) was completely different from what Jesus actually said and did and thought about himself.[1] According to Reimarus, Jesus and his disciples viewed him as the kind of messiah the Jews were expecting—a new king who would set up a temporal kingdom that redeemed all of Israel, and they believed this right up to the moment of his death.[2] Only after his death did the disciples change their view of Jesus from a temporal redeemer of the people of Israel to a suffering spiritual savior for all of human-kind, and the evangelists wrote their gospels from this new perspective. Reimarus writes, "Since they intended to present in the narrative their altered doctrine, they must have omitted zealously the things that led them to their earlier conclusions and must have written into the narrative in some detail the things from which their present doctrine is drawn."[3] In other words, the disciples invented from whole cloth the story of Jesus as a suffering savior who accomplishes spiritual salvation for all through his death on the cross. According to Reimarus, this belief was completely foreign to Jesus' own way of thinking. Like Jesus, the disciples had viewed him as an earthly king chosen by God to restore the kingdom of Israel. But the disciples "invented another doctrine concerning his intention, namely, of his becoming a suffering spiritual savior of men, only when their hopes had been disappointed after his death, and that they after-wards composed the narrative of his words and deeds. Consequently, this story and this doctrine are unfounded and false to this extent."[4] And so Reimarus completely rejected the understanding that Jesus died for the sins of all humanity as a story invented by the disciples to hide their disappointment and embarrassment that Jesus turned out not to be the king specially chosen by God, chalking it up to one of the ironies of history that this fabricated story eventually became the heart of Christian orthodoxy.

Fascinating (and compelling) as Reimarus' argument is, his view has certainly been held in the minority throughout centuries of Christian

1. In this way, Reimarus was extremely influential on the work of G. E. Lessing and other thinkers who first separated the Jesus of history from the Christ of faith, as well as on D. F. Strauss and others who embarked on the quest for the historical Jesus. See Talbert, introduction to *Reimarus*, 29–43.

2. Reimarus notes that even after Jesus' death, the apostles continue to describe their hopes about Jesus in terms of the earthly kingdom he would establish. See Luke 24:21: "We had hoped that he [Jesus of Nazareth] was the one to redeem Israel" (Reimarus, *Reimarus*, 127).

3. Ibid., 130.

4. Ibid., 134.

theology. The overwhelming majority of theologians and lay believers have affirmed that there is some sort of connection between Jesus' death and human salvation. Affirmations about who Jesus was (christological questions) and how he effects our salvation (soteriological questions) form the core of Christian belief. For centuries, theologians have been struggling to conceive and explain how God reconciles humanity to Godself through the life and death of Jesus, and they have proposed a multitude of different models and theories of atonement. Before we analyze these different theories, a bit of explanation about the concept of atonement will be helpful.

Atonement has several different meanings, but they all involve relationships and the righting of those relationships. Usually the word "atonement" is ascribed to William Tyndale,[5] an English scholar who was the first to translate the Bible directly from its original Hebrew and Greek into English. The story goes that Tyndale was working at translating the New Testament when he came across the concept we now call atonement, but that word didn't yet exist in the English language. So Tyndale made it up, and he did so by pushing together the words of its definition: *at-one-ment*. Simply put, atonement is the act or event that puts two parties back into the state of being at one with one another.

At the level of everyday conversation, atonement just means the action that repairs a broken relationship. An excellent example of this definition plays out in the movie *Atonement*, which was nominated for numerous Academy Awards in 2008. In the movie, a young girl accuses her older sister's lover of a crime he did not commit, for which he suffers horrible consequences. The story follows the girl as she grows up and tries desperately to repair her relationship with her sister and *atone* for the terrible deed she has committed. While not everyone may commit quite such a horrific misdeed, the need to right a wrong and repair a relationship is surely a common human experience. In this sense, atonement at the interpersonal level is surely a familiar concept.

Atonement, in the religious sense, carries the same idea but applies it to the relationship between humanity and God or the gods. Many of the world's religions have some concept of atonement—a ritual that makes amends for whatever the people have done to make the gods angry. The most common of these rituals is sacrifice, whether of humans, animals, crops, or similar valuables. Judaism, from biblical times through the

---

5. See McGrath, *Christian Literature*, 357; and Gillon, *Words to Trust*, 42.

Third Temple period, had an elaborate sacrificial system. A brief glance through Lev 1–7 reveals many instructions for how to make sacrifices, but it also shows that God is gracious and merciful because God provides a means by which the people's sins can be forgiven.[6] Thus, the overriding theological purpose of these sacrifices is to restore the people's relationship with this gracious and merciful God, but as the rabbi at B'Nai Abraham Zion pointed out, the purpose of such sacrifice was penance, not payment. Sacrifices repair this relationship because they express the Israelites' remorse for sin and their desire to be at one with God again.

As we move from a description of atonement in interpersonal relationships to human and divine relationships, the definition of atonement becomes more specific. In the religious definition, atonement involves particular rituals or actions. When we move to a specifically Christian definition of atonement, there is only one action that matters: the crucifixion of Christ. Many Christians have viewed Jesus as *the* sacrifice that repairs the relationship between God and humanity, but they have differed in their understanding of how that sacrifice atones for all of humanity. How exactly Jesus' sacrifice repairs the human-divine relationship and achieves atonement has been the subject of many subsequent theories of atonement, which we will analyze in detail in the following chapter.

But before we move to a discussion of those theories, something must be said in regards to Brethren theology, for this book sets out to construct a particularly Brethren view of atonement and salvation. The Church of the Brethren is a unique blend of the ideas of sixteenth-century Anabaptism and seventeenth-century Radical Pietism. Only the briefest of sketches is necessary here, however, for there are already many fine books that detail the history and theology of these movements.[7]

The major theories of atonement were already developed by the time of the Protestant Reformation that spawned both Anabaptism and Radical Pietism, but this period of reform brought questions of salvation (whether by works of the church or through grace by faith) to the forefront in a new and different way. The Anabaptist movement developed during the early years of the Protestant Reformation, and while the major contention between these radical Reformers and the magisterial

---

6. See Birch et al., *Introduction to the Old Testament*, 136. For a helpful description of the Temple complex, see Kraybill, *Kingdom*, 57–61.

7. For a history of Anabaptism, see Snyder, *Anabaptist History and Theology*. For a description of Pietism, see Brown, *Understanding Pietism*. For a history of the Church of the Brethren, see Durnbaugh, *Fruit of the Vine*; and Durnbaugh, *Believers' Church*.

Reformers was the issue of religious freedom from the state (as manifested in the debate over infant baptism), their understandings of salvation also differed. Anabaptists generally affirmed the doctrinal positions of the earlier radical Reformers, but the difference lay in the Anabaptist insistence upon linking faith and practice.

The telling of the Anabaptist story often begins with the baptisms of a group of radicals in Zürich, Switzerland. Until 1525, these radicals had been followers of Ulrich Zwingli and supporters of his reform movement in Zürich. However, they became frustrated by what they considered Zwingli's slow pace of reform. These radicals opposed Zwingli's decision to allow Zürich's city council to rule (in opposition to the radicals' views) on issues such as the tithe, images, the Mass, and anticlericalism in general, but the issue that finally pushed the radicals to break from Zwingli was baptism.[8] The radicals rejected the validity of infant baptism. They believed that infants do not have the capacity for the faith required for baptism—that only those who had heard the gospel, desired to live a new life of discipleship, and requested baptism for themselves should be baptized. When the Zürich City Council decreed in January 1525 that all infants must be baptized, the group of radicals led by Conrad Grebel, Felix Mantz, and George Blaurock met for discussion in Mantz's home. There they decided that they could not abide by the council's ruling, and on that night, they baptized one another into what would eventually become known as the Anabaptist ("re-baptizer") movement. The radicals rejected the name of "re-baptizer" because they considered their own baptisms as infants to be meaningless. Because this adult baptism was their only legitimate baptism, they did not believe they were *re*-baptized. Instead, they called themselves simply "Brethren."

Although the Swiss Anabaptists are often held up as the defining group of the early Anabaptist movement,[9] there were other Anabaptist groups forming in other parts of Europe around the same time.[10]

---

8. Until 1523, Zwingli himself may have had some doubts about the validity of infant baptism. If, according to the Protestant claim, salvation is by grace through faith and grace is not conferred by sacraments, it is curious that Zwingli would insist on infant baptism. Similarly, Zwingli's own spiritualized view of the sacraments would seem to negate the need for infant baptism.

9. See, for example, Bender, "Anabaptist Vision," 72–73.

10. Until around 1975, the consensus among scholars of Anabaptism (led by Harold S. Bender) was that the Anabaptist movement began in Zurich in 1525 with the baptism of these men and women in Felix Mantz's house. They believed that the movement then spread across Germany and parts of Europe as members of these early

Anabaptism in South Germany and Austria had a different flavor than the Anabaptist movement in Switzerland. Whereas Anabaptism in Switzerland arose in opposition to Zwingli's slow pace of reform, Anabaptism in South Germany and Austria was shaped by the failed Peasants' War of 1525 and was influenced by the apocalyptic theology of Thomas Müntzer.[11] In general, Anabaptism in this area was more mystical than Swiss Anabaptism, and it focused more on the work of the Spirit within individual believers than on ethical discipleship in the model of Jesus. Anabaptists in this stream had lively apocalyptic expectations, and because they did not place as much emphasis on nonresistance or pacifism as the Swiss did, they were more willing to take up arms to usher in the imminent kingdom of God.

Despite the remarkable differences between early Anabaptist leaders, there soon emerged a set of core convictions that most later Anabaptists professed, and this set of convictions seems to have been influenced more strongly by Swiss Anabaptism than the other streams of Anabaptist thought.[12] The core conviction that most concerns us here is the way they understood salvation.

At the heart of Anabaptist soteriology is the conviction that salvation necessarily includes an ethical component. Anabaptists agreed that salvation was by grace, but they refused to say that it was "by faith alone." Instead, they understood that "the faith that leads to salvation is a faith that bears visible fruit in repentance, conversion, regeneration, obedience, and a new life dedicated to the love of God and the neighbor, by the power of the Holy Spirit. In other words, true faith leads to discipleship" and a necessarily visible church.[13] Although the mainline or magisterial

---

Swiss Brethren moved about, spread their faith, and won converts to Anabaptism. However, after publication of the landmark article "From Monogenesis to Polygenesis" by Strayer et al., scholars began to conclude that there was not just one birthplace of Anabaptism. Rather, pockets of Anabaptism seemed to spring up almost simultaneously across Germany.

11. For a more detailed history of the South German and Austrian stream of Anabaptists, see Snyder, *Anabaptist History and Theology*, 121–24.

12. The Anabaptist theology that influenced later Brethren leaders was certainly the Swiss variety. Dale Stoffer argues that the so-called Mennonites that Alexander Mack knew in the Palatinate were most likely Swiss Brethren rather than Dutch Mennonite (Stoffer, "Swiss Brethren," 29–30).

13. Snyder, *Anabaptist History and Theology*, 151. Here they disagreed with Augustine, who believed that the true church (those who have been saved) is invisible because only God can know for sure (Augustine, *City of God, passim*). The Anabaptists believed that a person's inner salvation is necessarily reflected in his or her outer life,

Reformers also affirmed that an ethical life followed being made right before God, the Anabaptists stressed more strongly the connection between the inner life of faith and the outward life of discipleship and affirmed that both are necessary for salvation. For example, one anonymous early Anabaptist author wrote that Christ's satisfaction is efficacious only for those who live the Christian life, including self-denial, good works, and cross-bearing.[14] In other words, they believed that salvation by grace through faith was conditional, and salvation can never be separated from ethics.

To be sure, the magisterial Reformers also emphasized the necessity of an ethical life. However, they affirmed that an ethical life *follows* justification before God. For Luther and Melanchthon, "good works had a role in the plan of salvation in terms of the Christian's relationship with his neighbors but not in terms of the relationship between God and man. They [good works] do not add to Christ's work for our redemption, but emerge out of man's gratitude for his unmerited salvation, and benefit his fellow man."[15] In contrast, the Anabaptists insisted that *both* faith and discipleship are necessary for salvation. In other words, right believing or good faith is impossible without right living, for based on the assumption of this connection between inner faith and outward life, an unethical life would be a reflection of inadequate faith. Many Anabaptists illustrate this idea with a well-known story. An Amish or Brethren or Mennonite man (depending on who tells the story) was once approached by an evangelist who asked whether he was saved. After thinking for a moment, the man replied, "Go ask my hired man, my banker, my feed salesman, my neighbors, and members of my family. See what they have to say."[16] The point, of course, is that salvation is not just about the individual; it has real, lived effects.

Salvation, and the discipleship that is necessarily a part of it, was not just about individual discipline; it was a way of life in the world that affected the whole community. In this way, there is a communal element

---

such that the true church is indeed visible. Thus, anyone can tell who has been saved simply by looking at Christians' lives.

14. Friedmann, *Theology of Anabaptism*, 84. Friedmann adds that "not only the isolated event at Calvary alone, but the cross that every believer faces when consistently living a life of discipleship is what works toward salvation" (ibid., 85).

15. Depperman and Drewery, *Hoffman*, 238.

16. See Hauerwas, "Testament of Friends," 212; and Kraybill and Eisenbise, *Brethren in a Postmodern World*, 14.

to salvation. Unlike the Lutheran and Reformed views that taught that salvation is a result of individual belief, Anabaptists found that a person cannot be saved without caring for his or her sister and brother. Menno-nite theologian Robert Friedman writes, "It is not 'faith alone' which mat-ters . . . but it is brotherhood, this intimate caring for each other, as it was commanded to the disciples of Christ as the way to God's kingdom."[17] He argues, "All individualism and individualistic concern for personal salva-tion is ruled out. No one can enter the kingdom [of God] except together with his brother . . . The horizontal man-to-man relationship belongs to the kingdom just as much as does the vertical God-man relationship. In fact, the belief prevails that one cannot come to God (that is, attain salva-tion) except as one comes to Him together with one's brother."[18]

In this way, the early Anabaptists embraced a "kingdom theology" in contrast to a theology whose primary concern is personal salvation: "Kingdom theology does not mean merely a glorious expectation of life after death to be reached by the pious and ascetic; it means a radical turn in life itself, the breaking in of a new dimension into the physical ex-istence of man."[19] In other words, for Anabaptists, salvation is not just about individuals and their after-death rewards; it is also here and now, it is lived, and it is relational. Thus, Anabaptist soteriology is concerned about service to others.

The other branch of Brethren spiritual heritage comes from the Rad-ical Pietist movement. Pietism was a reform movement that began in the German Lutheran Church in the late seventeenth century as a reaction to Protestant scholasticism.[20] After the Reformation, the Lutheran Church quickly became concerned with the intellectual formation of correct doctrines, developing the understanding that salvation is achieved by as-sent to correct doctrine.[21] The Pietists, led initially by Philip Jacob Spener and his student, August Hermann Franke, rejected this idea because they believed that Christianity in general and salvation in particular is about more than doctrine or intellectual agreement. They believed that it must

17. Friedmann, "On Mennonite Historiography," 121.

18. Ibid., "Doctrine of the Two Worlds," 112–13.

19. Ibid., 113–14.

20. Another important influence on the rise of Pietism was the economic hardship and moral decadence spawned by the Thirty Years' War. See Gordon, "Pietism and the Brethren," lines 1–7, for a full description of the war's influence on the movement.

21. For a complete description of the early Pietist movement, see Herzog, Euro-pean Pietism Reviewed.

also entail some sort of reformation of life.[22] Pietists were concerned with morality and the lives of real Christians, and they claimed that correct doctrine does not make a bit of difference in these areas.[23] That is, Pietists thought Lutheran orthodoxy placed too much emphasis on purity of doctrine and not enough emphasis on purity of life, too much emphasis on the head and not enough on the heart. Spener himself wrote that "it is by no means enough to have knowledge of the Christian faith, for Christianity consists rather of practice."[24]As such, Pietists emphasized a theology of experience, specifically in the areas of repentance, the new birth, and conversion. Whereas Lutheran orthodoxy focused on salvation, and especially on the idea that salvation is a gift of grace from God, Pietists were more concerned with what happened after the moment of salvation: regeneration and sanctification. In this way, Pietism shifted the focus from salvation to "the moral obligation of the saved."[25]

Spener and Francke did not dismiss the power of sin or the inability of humans to save themselves.[26] However, they did emphasize that Christ works in and through humans in order to produce works of righteousness and obedience. In fact, Spener argued that good works necessarily follow from faith, as if they are a necessary part of salvation.[27] Furthermore, they are understood as a crucial component of the process of sanctification, the process by which the Holy Spirit makes a person holy.

Pietism is often accused of rejecting the world and its pleasures in favor of strict asceticism and hard work.[28] However, as Brethren theologian Dale Brown points out, Spener and Francke did not reject worldly pleasures because they thought they were inherently evil; instead, they preached that Christians should not waste their time with frivolities and should remain focused on glorifying God and helping the neighbor.[29] The important point is that Pietists did not hate or reject the goodness

---

22. See Brown, *Understanding Pietism*, 83. Marcus Meier states it well in explaining that the Pietists tried to anchor piety in the experiences of the individual (Meier, "Brethren," 114).

23. Nagler, *Pietism and Methodism*, 22.

24. Spener, *Pia Desideria*, 95.

25. Brown, *Understanding Pietism*, 84.

26. See Jennings, *Two Discourses*, 72–73; and Spener, *Pia Desideria*, 63.

27. Brown, *Understanding Pietism*, 93–94.

28. See Wildenhahn, *Spener*, 28–29; and Weber, *Protestant Ethic*, 62.

29. Brown, *Understanding Pietism*, 126.

of the material world. In fact, they believed that their salvation rested at least in part on their care for that world.

Though there were certainly points of tension between Pietists and the leaders of the Lutheran Church in Germany, it was never Spener's or Francke's intention to break away from the church and form a new denomination. Their intention was always to reform the church from within rather than to split from it. There were others within the movement, however, who had more separatist leanings. Like Zwingli's radical followers in Switzerland, these people were frustrated by the slow pace of Pietist reform. They were heavily influenced by the writings of Jakob Boehme, a seventeenth-century German Christian mystic, as well as those of German Lutheran theologian Gottfried Arnold. Convinced by Boehme's caustic critique of the institutional church and by Arnold's claim that the true church has always existed outside of the institutional church in so-called heretical Christian movements, these Radical Pietists decided that they must separate from the church, for "they came to believe that leaders like Spener and Francke compromised with the evils of the day and depended too much on the church's institutional framework."[30] Clearly, this radical branch of Pietism contained an inherent wariness of the established church.

We can see several important connections between Anabaptist theology and that of Radical Pietism, especially in the area of discipleship or reformation of life, but they became most fully woven together in the Church of the Brethren. Radical Pietism emerged on the heels of Anabaptism in most of what is now Germany, and it often took root in areas where some of the Anabaptist zeal had faded. This was the case in the Palatinate, the area where Alexander Mack lived.[31] He invited Ernst Hochmann von Hochenau, a famous Pietist evangelist, to his town to preach the tenets of Radical Pietism there. One of those tenets was a complete rejection of the corrupted and institutional church—indeed, any form of institutional church. The Radical Piests believed that a church community was unnecessary for a believer to know God and live well.

Mack and Hochmann were close friends, but they eventually became estranged when Mack and the other early Brethren decided that in order to really follow Christ's teachings in all things, they needed a

30. Durnbaugh, *Fruit of the Vine*, 10.

31. Marcus Meier provides an excellent account of the interplay between Anabaptism and Pietism in the Palatinate, including numerous contacts Mack likely had with Anabaptist neighbors (Meier, "Brethren," 117–18).

church community. The early Brethren realized that it would be impossible to have communion without a gathered body. Hochmann felt that this was an unfortunate fall back into the institutionalized error they had found in the state churches, and so he and Mack went their separate ways.

Although the early Brethren came out of Radical Pietism, when they decided to form their own church community, they patterned themselves on the Anabaptists.[32] Because of this, Brethren historian Donald Durnbaugh writes that the best way to understand Brethren is as a Radical Pietist group that appropriated an Anabaptist view of church.[33]

It should be clear by this point that although Anabaptism and Pietism arose in different milieus and in response to different stimuli, there are obvious points of connection between the two theologies, especially in regards to their soteriological views, and the early Brethren managed to pull together these common threads. Both groups were concerned with the fruits of salvation, believing that it is not enough to rest in the assurance of salvation; people must necessarily live out that salvation by doing good works and helping the neighbor in need. Both groups also recognized the importance of the community—not only because the community was the bastion of support during times of persecution, but also because their understandings of salvation necessarily included a social or communal element.

Another important point of commonality between the Anabaptists and (Radical) Pietists was their fairly optimistic view of humanity. They had a much more positive theological anthropology than did the mainline Reformers. Anabaptists were able to demand lives of discipleship from their members because they believed humans maintain the capacity to do good. In this way, the Anabaptist view of humanity was much closer to the medieval Catholic view than it was to the mainstream Protestant understanding that humanity is depraved and unable to stop sinning. Anabaptists believed that humanity has the capacity to respond to God's

---

32. In most cases, the Brethren patterned their communal ordinances on the Anabaptist example. The one exception was baptism. Immersion baptism was the one rite that Radical Pietists found legitimate because it seemed to be the practice of the earliest Christians. The Brethren derived their baptismal practice from the Pietists rather than the Anabaptists, and this is why Brethren baptize using three-fold immersion forward rather than pouring, like the Mennonites (ibid., "Brethren," 125).

33. Durnbaugh and Bowman, *Church of the Brethren*, 4. It is interesting to note that Brethren ecclesiology reflects the more congregational approach of the Swiss Brethren rather than the bishop/minister pattern of the Mennonites. See Stoffer, "Swiss Brethren," 33–34.

call for regeneration and therefore has both the capacity and responsibility to live disciplined lives of discipleship following Jesus' model. After all, they reasoned, Jesus would not have issued any ethical commandments if he didn't think humans had the capacity to follow those commandments.

Likewise, Anabaptists were not as influenced by Augustine's notion of original sin as were other Protestants, and this is one of the reasons they rejected the practice of infant baptism. Their primary objection to infant baptism was that infants are incapable of expressing the belief and commitment necessary for baptism to have any meaning, but they also denied the claim that infants are tainted by original sin and therefore sacrifice salvation if they are not baptized. In his "Basic Questions," Alexander Mack flatly denies that children forfeit their salvation as long as they are not baptized. He writes, "The baptism commanded of believers does not concern children before they are able to profess their faith . . . Salvation is not dependent upon the water, but only upon the faith, which must be proved by love and obedience."[34] Though Mack's emphasis is on the adult profession of faith necessary for baptism, the implication is that baptism is not necessary to wipe away original sin. In general, Anabaptists did not write much about original sin or the fall; their view was focused much more clearly on the requirements of discipleship for the here and now. They did not necessarily deny the problem of sin, but their theology did not dwell on it. Thus, although Anabaptists did affirm that humanity is saved *from* something, such as sin, death, hell, etc., they also insisted that humanity is saved *for* something as well. In this way, they had a higher view of the nature of saved humanity. Whereas Luther maintained that humans are simply imputed righteous for Christ's sake, the Anabaptists thought that being saved meant becoming actually righteous by the power of the Holy Spirit.[35] Therefore, they believed that humans do have the ability to truly obey Jesus' commandments and live lives of radical discipleship based on Jesus' Sermon on the Mount teachings and his way in the world.

Pietists shared this confidence in the capacity of humanity to be restored to goodness. They "maintained that the God who is good enough to forgive sin is powerful enough to transform the sinner."[36] Without this assurance, Pietists worried that the doctrine of original sin would

---

34. Mack, "Basic Questions," 30–32.

35. Snyder, *Anabaptist History and Theology*, 61–62.

36. Brown, *Understanding Pietism*, 89.

be used as an excuse for not bettering one's life. In response to criticism for preaching that Christians should strive for perfection, Spener writes, "We are not forbidden to seek perfection, but we are urged toward it . . . even if we shall never in this life achieve such a degree of perfection . . . we are nevertheless under obligation to achieve some degree of perfection."[37] Though Pietists maintained the orthodox Lutheran position that Christ's righteousness is imputed, they argued that this idea must be balanced by the fact that Christ works in and through Christians as well.[38] In other words, it is not enough to simply assent to some doctrines and have faith that Christ's death has somehow redeemed all of humanity. Both the early Anabaptists and Pietists—and therefore the early Brethren as well—believed that there is more to Christianity and the Christian understanding of salvation than that. All of these groups demanded a radical life of discipleship in community and in response to the neighbor in need as both the result of and as a necessary ingredient for salvation.

This book has twin focal points: atonement theory and Brethren soteriology. This chapter has sought to provide an introduction to both of those ideas by explaining what Christians mean by atonement and what makes historical Brethren soteriology unique. The following chapters will build on these ideas as we alternate between the two topics. To that end, chapter 2 devotes itself to the idea of atonement by examining the most popular theories and models that have been proposed throughout Christian history.

---

37. Spener, *Pia Desideria*, 80.

38. Ibid.

CHAPTER 2

Traditional Models of Atonement

For centuries, Christians have been seeking to understand how the life and death of Jesus as the Christ saves humanity. Most of them have affirmed that somehow Jesus puts God and humanity back in right relationship—at one. Over the past two thousand years, theologians have proposed many different theories or models in an effort to explain just how Jesus does that. All of these models begin with the assumption that humanity is somehow alienated from God and that God repairs that alienation through the work of Christ. Some of these models enjoyed great popularity for centuries; others were only relevant for a short period of time. In general, these models are contextually-bound. The theologians who proposed them were doing their best to make Jesus' death and God's saving work sensible in terms of their own worldviews. As such, some of these models may seem ridiculous to modern readers, but it is important to keep in mind that each of these theories was meaningful to Christians at certain points in history.

We can group most of the major historical atonement theories into seven models that describe what Jesus does to give him soteriological significance: sacrifice, victor (as recapitulator, as restorer/deifier, and as ransom), satisfaction, exemplar, and substitute. We will explore each of these seven models in turn, noting when and by whom the model was proposed, how it functions, and its advantages and critiques.

Sacrifice

Of all the atonement models, the idea of Christ as sacrifice is perhaps the oldest. This model was proposed by the writer of the Letter to the Hebrews, and it draws on the sacrificial system used in the Old Testament.[1] This author was undoubtedly influenced by the surrounding Jewish culture, liturgy, and sacrificial system, which used sacrifices to cleanse a person from unrighteousness or to seal a covenant.[2] But Jesus' function as a sacrifice in the Letter to the Hebrews is much greater, because he is greater than a mere animal:

> For if the blood of goats and bulls, with the sprinkling of the ashes of a heifer, sanctifies those who have been defiled so that their flesh is purified, how much more will the blood of Christ, who through the eternal Spirit offered himself without blemish to God, purify our conscience from dead works to worship the living God! For this reason he is the mediator of a new covenant, so that those who are called may receive the promised eternal inheritance, because a death has occurred that redeems them from the transgressions under the first covenant (Heb 9:13–15).

There are two important points contained in this passage. The first is that Christ's sacrifice is greater and more beneficial than the sacrifice of an animal because it has a greater effect. It offers eternal redemption rather than just removal of impurity or atonement of sin (Heb 9:9–12). The second point is that Christ's sacrifice is greater and more beneficial because it is the last necessary sacrifice. Because Christ's sacrifice was so perfect, it did not need to be offered again and again every year on the Day of Atonement. As the epistle author states repeatedly, this sacrifice is made once and for all. He writes, "But as it is, he has appeared once and for all at the end of the age to remove sin by the sacrifice of himself" (Heb

1. This model is alluded to in other New Testament passages as well, most notably Mark 14:22–25, John 1:29, and Rom 3:25, but it is developed most fully in Hebrews. Several early theologians made use of this model as well, especially Cyprian and Tertullian. See Tertullian, "Against the Jews," 156–58, 164–68; and Ep. lxii to Caecilius in Cyprian, *Writings of Cyprian*, 208–221. Although Cyprian's immediate focus in this epistle is proper Eucharistic ritual, the theology that guides his understanding of what makes a proper ritual is his understanding of Christ as sacrifice.

2. McIntyre, *Shape of Soteriology*, 34. However, it is important to note that the understanding of how a sacrifice atones or purifies a person of sin had undergone some significant development in the early church. Early Christians were not using the term in precisely the same way that it had previously functioned in the Jewish understanding (Schmiechen, *Saving Power*, 21–23).

9:26b). Similarly, "And it is by God's will that we have been sanctified through the offering of the body of Jesus Christ once for all" (Heb 10:10). Therefore, Jesus' sacrifice of himself supersedes and negates the need for any future sacrifice.

But in the Letter to the Hebrews, Jesus does not just act as the perfect sacrifice; he is also the priest who offers the perfect sacrifice. In this way, he also supersedes and negates the need for any future priestly system. As the perfect priest, Christ opens up new access to God by supplanting the old covenant/Law and creating a new covenant. Over and over again, the author identifies a point of commonality between Jesus and the Levitical priesthood, but then claims that Jesus does away with this system. For example, he writes, "But Jesus has now obtained a more excellent ministry, and to that degree he is the mediator of a better covenant, which has been enacted through better promises. For if that first covenant had been faultless, there would have been no need to look for a second one" (Heb 8:6–7). The author believes that Jesus has somehow broken with the old system and instituted something new and better. As theologian Peter Schmiechen points out, "Jesus surpasses the Levitical priesthood in authority, permanence, and sanctification by faith."[3]

As a sacrifice, Jesus puts humanity in right relationship by offering his own blood to cover the sins of humanity. This idea has a direct correlation with the Jewish understanding of a sin offering, the point of which was to remove the stain of sin. Jews understood that the option of sacrifice was a gift given by God to purify them and put them back into relationship with the community; the point was absolutely not to appease God's anger over sin.[4] Therefore, in this model, the object of the atoning action is the offending sin, not God, and not necessarily even the person who committed the sin. Covering or removing the sin purifies the sinner, and it is only as a result of the removal of this sin that the sinner is restored to right relationship with his or her neighbors and also with God.

Understanding Jesus' atoning death as a sacrifice has several advantages. First, it highlights Christianity's descent from Judaism. It offered

---

3. Ibid., 33.

4. Sin offerings purify the sinner; they are not exchanges between sinner and God. Smiechen writes, "The sin offering must be seen in the context of the general view of sin itself. As a violation of covenantal law, sin breaks relation with God and other people. As a break in harmonious relations, it is seen as a stain or contagion that infects the person and the entire community. Therefore there is the need for purification. To be sure, the broken relation must be restored, but sin itself is a burden that must be removed" (ibid., 21). In other words, the sin offering benefits the sinner, not God.

the earliest Jewish Christians an understanding of Jesus' horrible death in a way that made use of their established theological framework and cultic rituals. That is to say, it was not a difficult mental leap to understand Jesus as a part of the sacrificial system.

A second key advantage of this model is that it seems to be located in the bedrock of Christian theology. Not only is this model present in the Letter to the Hebrews, a first-century text that the church valued enough to include in the canon, but the idea of Jesus as a sacrifice has also been important in the liturgy from almost the very beginning of the Christian tradition. The notion that Jesus died as a sacrifice to all is almost inescapable in the celebration of the Eucharist. Though eucharistic theology sometimes includes the non-sacrificial themes of the *Didache*,[5] the view that Jesus understood his own death as an atoning sacrifice (as indicated by his words of institution at the Last Supper) prevails in most liturgical practices. Therefore, the sacrifice model provides an advantage for contemporary believers because it links us to ancient traditions—both Christian and Jewish traditions.

Despite these important advantages, understanding Jesus' death as a sacrifice does not seem fully adequate or satisfactory. For one thing, the idea is clearly supersessionist in claiming the new covenant instituted by Christ replaces the old covenant between God and Jews. This clearly was not problematic for the writer of the Letter to the Hebrews, since that was his main point about Jesus. However, for many contemporary Christians, the supersessionist idea that Christianity replaces Judaism is uncomfortable because it carries the notion that "Jews by their sins, most prominently their sin of rejecting Jesus as the Messiah, have forfeited any covenantal status."[6] In other words, this kind of theology asserts that Christianity is the fullest articulation of God's plan for the world and that it offers more direct access to God than does Judaism. Given the history of anti-Semitism in the church, which supersessionist theology has often been used to justify, many contemporary Christians are rightly wary of any kind of understanding that reveres Jesus and his death while denigrating the Jewish religion from which he came.[7]

---

5. See Eisenbise, "Come to the Table," 51–56.

6. Novak, "Covenant in Rabbinic Thought," 66.

7. Elisabeth Schüssler Fiorenza offers a compelling argument for why Christians should be wary of highlighting the differences between Jesus and his Jewish background. See Schüssler Fiorenza, *In Memory of Her*, 105–108.

In this sacrificial model of atonement, the sacrifice cleanses and purifies the sinner, therefore returning him or her to right relationship and status in the community. As discussed earlier, that sin offering does not affect God or how God views the sinner. The offering does not appease God's anger, yet this distinction is often blurred in later uses of this model. Later theories make use of the understanding of Jesus as sacrifice, but they locate that understanding within larger frameworks that depict God as a wrathful and abusive being who displays no mercy, as we will see in our discussion of ransom, satisfaction, and substitute. While the later misuse of this model is not necessarily a critique of the model of sacrifice itself, it does point out that contemporary believers (both Christians and Jews) are so far removed from the Temple sacrificial system that the nuances of this model are lost. It may be that this understanding of Jesus as sacrifice has been co-opted and ruined by later theories.

Christ as Victor

Another early Christian belief was that Jesus offers salvation by defeating the powers of sin, death, and hell. This idea is firmly ensconced in many of the favorite hymns still sung in churches on Easter Sunday:

> Thine is the glory, risen conqu'ring Son!
> Endless is the vict'ry thou o'er death hast won.
> Angels in bright raiment rolled the stone away,
> kept the folded grave-clothes where thy body lay.
> Thine is the glory, risen, conqu'ring Son!
> Endless is the vict'ry thou o'er death hast won.[8]

Consider too:

> Up from the grave he arose,
> with a mighty triumph o'er his foes!
> He arose a victor from the dark domain,
> and he lives forever with his saints to reign!
> He arose! He arose! Alleluia! Christ arose![9]

The view that Jesus' death is somehow a triumph and victory over humanity's enemies continues to be meaningful to many Christians

8. Budry, "Thine Is the Glory," 269.
9. Lowry, "Low in the Grave He Lay," 273.

today, just as it was to the earliest Christians. It is for this reason that this Christ the Victor (often known by its Latin name, *Christus Victor*) model is referred to as the "classic" theory of atonement.[10] Many theologians have employed this model, including the Apostle Paul, Origen, Irenaeus, Cyprian, Augustine, Athanasius, and Martin Luther, but they use the model in different ways.

As the name of this theory suggests, it views Christ as one who fights against and triumphs over the evil powers of the world. As such, it is not a systematic theory, but more of a drama or passion story of God: "Its central theme is the idea of the Atonement as a Divine conflict and victory; Christ—*Christus Victor*—fights against and triumphs over the evil powers of the world, the 'tyrants' under which mankind is in bondage and suffering, and in Him God reconciles the world to Himself."[11] The plot of the drama is this: The cosmos is in a constant battle between the forces of God and Satan. In that battle, God's Son Jesus was killed, which seemed like a victory for Satan and a defeat of God. But by Jesus' resurrection, that apparent defeat was transformed into a great victory, "which forever established God's control of the universe and freed sinful humans from the power of sin and Satan."[12] In this model, salvation and atonement are not separated. Atonement is an objective triumph over sin, death, and the devil. Salvation is a victory that Christ has gained once and for all and is continued in the work of the Holy Spirit. In this model, the work of salvation is entirely God's (through Christ), and it brings about a complete change in the world and in the situation of humanity. However, the model does not fully explain how that change happens. Therefore, early theologians expanded on this basic story by developing a variety of theories that tried to fill in the details. The three most important of these sub-theories in the *Christus Victor* category are Christ as recapitulator, Christ as restorer, and Christ as ransom.

---

10. Aulén argues that this Christ the Victor theory of atonement was the dominant model in the church for at least the first century and was only replaced when Anselm introduced his satisfaction model (Aulén, *Christus Victor*, 22–23).

11. Ibid., 20.

12. Weaver, *Nonviolent Atonement*, 15.

Recapitulation

The theory of recapitulation was proposed by Irenaeus, Bishop of Lyons, who lived and wrote during the second century. Like the other theories in the *Christus Victory* category, Irenaeus believed that through his life, death, and resurrection, Christ somehow defeated the powers that hold humanity in bondage. This theory differs, however, in that it stresses what Jesus did throughout his entire life span, including his birth, life, death, resurrection, and ascension. According to Irenaeus, all of humanity is united insofar as we all are the recipients of Adam's sin and are therefore all in bondage to Satan. This bondage keeps creation from developing the way God intended. God designed us to continue to grow in maturity, insight, and communication with the divine, but sin and bondage derailed that plan.[13] Therefore, humanity needs a liberator to free us from that bondage and allow us to bloom into the creatures God intended us to be. For Irenaeus, Jesus was that liberator, and he liberated humanity by living the perfect life and thus undoing Adam's sin. Whereas Adam lived a life of disobedience and therefore trapped all of his descendants in bondage to Satan and those powers that keep humanity from developing a full relationship with God, Jesus lived a life of perfect obedience by acting obediently where Adam acted disobediently. In this way, Jesus re-lives Adam's life, undoing his sin. He *recapitulates* and annuls Adam's sin, which restores and perfects creation. Irenaeus explains it well: "But when he was incarnate and made man, he recapitulated in himself the long line of the human race, procuring for us salvation thus summarily, so that what we had lost in Adam, that is, the being in the image and likeness of God, that we should regain in Christ Jesus."[14] Furthermore, under this view, Jesus' experience of each stage of human life offers an example for every person to follow, regardless of his or her age or station in life.[15]

According to Irenaeus, Jesus puts humanity and God back into right relationship by undoing human sin. He becomes a man just like Adam was, subject to all human frailties, but whereas Adam was overcome by the powers of evil, Jesus was not. In some ways, then, Jesus' life is like a

---

13. Gonález, *Christian Thought Revisited*, 57. It is important to note that Irenaeus did not think that development and growth of the human species was bad or the result of sin. Rather, it is the form that growth and development has taken that is the result of sin. He thought that even if humanity had not sinned, the incarnation still would have occurred, for it was always part of God's plan (Irenaeus, *Against Heresies*, 295).

14. Ibid., 275.

15. Ibid., 159.

new creation or a re-creation, which is why Irenaeus referred to him as the New Adam. Humanity participates in this new creation because we share Jesus' humanity, just like we share Adam's humanity. When Jesus was resurrected, he destroyed the powers of death and sin and opened for his followers a "gap through which we too can escape from bondage."[16] In this way, humanity's union with Christ plays an important part in this theory. We are part of the re-creation because we are united with Christ and share his victory over the powers of sin and death. Irenaeus viewed this union of the human and divine as the center of Christ's work,[17] but it was Athanasius, a third-century saint, who developed this idea more fully in his restorer model.

Restoration/Deification

Like Irenaeus, Athanasius viewed the goal of salvation as the renewal of creation. He affirms that creation is good, but it is still external to and removed from God. Because creation is separated from God, it is therefore subject to corruption and change.[18] Accordingly, although humanity was created in God's image and given a portion of God's power so that we might forever abide in blessedness, we rejected God and things eternal. As a result of this rejection, death gained a legal hold over humanity because God had laid down the law that we would suffer mortality as a result of our rejection of God, and as a result, corruptibility entered human nature.[19] Although the sin is itself grievous, it seems that the introduction of corruptibility is even worse. Athanasius argues that if it were merely a matter of transgression, repentance for the sin would be sufficient. However, human nature was corrupted to the point that it no longer reflected the image of God. Therefore, salvation is not just about forgiveness of guilt or sins, for "God could have wiped out our guilt, had He so pleased, by a word: but human nature required to be healed, restored, *recreated*.[20]

According to Athanasius, God had already determined that human rejection of the divine would lead to the loss of immortality and a corrupted relationship with God:

16. Gonález, *Christian Thought Revisited*, 59.

17. Ibid., 61.

18. Lyman, *Christology and Cosmology*, 141.

19. Athanasius, *On the Incarnation*, 57–61.

20. Robertson, introduction to *Athanasius de Incarnatione*, xx.

> For bringing them into his own paradise, he [God] gave them a law, so that if they guarded the grace and remained good, they might have the life of paradise—without sorrow, pain, or care—besides having the promise of their incorruptibility in heaven; but if they were to transgress and turning away become wicked, they would know themselves enduring the corruption of death according to nature, and no longer live in paradise, but thereafter dying outside of it, would remain in death and corruption. This also the Divine Scripture foretells, speaking in the person of God, "You may eat from all the trees in paradise; from the tree of knowledge of good and evil you shall not eat. On the day you eat of it, you shall die by death" (Gen 2:16–18). This "you shall die by death," what else might it be except not merely to die, but to remain in the corruption of death?[21]

As part of the plan of creation, God instituted this law of death, and once humanity transgressed and rejected God, God could not simply overturn this law of punishment because to do so would prove the divine word false. Yet neither could a good and merciful God allow humanity to just fester in ruin.[22] Therefore, out of love for humanity, God decided to renew creation through the incarnation of the Word, who was, after all, the one through whom God made everything in the beginning.[23] Because of sin and our corrupted nature, humans do not have the capability to know God, so the Word took on a human body so that humanity may recognize God. But to completely restore the divine-human relationship, people must do more than simply recognize God; they must be reunited with God.

So it is that God wants to be in relationship with humanity, but the only way humans can know and relate to God is through a restoration of our divine image. Through the incarnation, Christ takes on human nature in order to recreate it. All of human nature is taken on and up by Christ's incarnation. When human nature was fused with divine nature in the incarnation, it changed human nature forever by allowing it to participate in a transforming, divine relationship. It is important to note that the Word takes on flesh in order to effect a whole transformation of human nature, not just human behavior. For Athanasius, then, what keeps humanity separated from God is not disobedience, but rather our

---

21. Athanasius, *On the Incarnation*, 57.

22. Ibid., 65.

23. Ibid., 65–67.

fallen human nature, while what puts humanity and God back at one is the divinization of human nature. Divinization of human nature does not mean that humans become God or even become like God. Instead, it means that we participate in a transforming relationship with God that allows a certain sharing in God's power.[24]

Clearly, the incarnation plays a key role in Athanasius' theory of atonement, but he does not completely ignore the role of Jesus' death—especially his death on a cross. Athanasius argues that when divinity was fused with a human body in the incarnation, that body became incorruptible, such that two things occurred simultaneously: "the death of all was completed in the lordly body, and also death and corruption were destroyed by the Word in it."[25] That is to say that Christ's death fulfilled the requirement that death and corruption result from the original transgression (what Athanasius calls "the law of death"[26]), but after accepting this death, he is resurrected, which demonstrates his great power, even over death itself.

Athanasius believed Christ's death on a *cross* was necessary for several reasons. First, it was a public execution, which showed that Christ did not die from natural causes (which could make it seem that Christ had succumbed to natural weakness). The public nature of his death allowed all to see that he really was dead so they would therefore believe in his resurrection.[27] Second, the cross was necessary to show that Christ was powerful to defeat any kind of death, not just one of his own choosing. Otherwise, "it would provide the suspicion against him that he was not powerful over every form of death but only concerning that which he devised, and then the pretext for disbelief regarding the resurrection would again be no less."[28]

Christ's death is also necessary because it leads to the resurrection. Athanasius argues that just as the divine Word was joined to human nature in the incarnation, so too must human nature be taken into divinity. As the two are joined, so humans share in Christ's resurrection. They are also assured of their own resurrection so that they need no longer fear

24. Lyman, *Christology and Cosmology*, 158. By way of explanation, Lyman writes, "The body of Christ thus allows other human bodies to be temples of God, because it has stabilized the physical weakness which is the product of sin" (ibid.).

25. Athanasius, *On the Incarnation*, 95.

26. Ibid., 63.

27. Ibid., 99–101.

28. Ibid., 101–103.

death. In other words, Christ's resurrection was the first fruits of what Christians can expect themselves. Through the incarnation (and as illustrated by the death and resurrection), Christ has recreated the whole of human nature from corruption to incorruption and from death to immortality; Christ has recreated humanity's divine image and restored the relationship between humanity and God.

Ransom

Christ as ransom was another early model that the church fathers used to explain Christ's death. Origen was the first to suggest this idea that Christ offers himself to ransom us from death, but Gregory of Nyssa most vividly illustrated this theory through his fish-hook analogy. Gregory, a fourth-century Cappadocian theologian, argued that once Adam bartered away his freedom to the devil by succumbing to temptation and eating the fruit in the garden, Satan gained legal rights over humanity. Once Satan became the legal master of humanity, God could not arbitrarily remove people from the devil's grasp.[29] God's own justice demands that God respect Satan's rights. Therefore, Christ takes on human flesh while still displaying some divine capabilities (such as performing miracles). In this way, Christ's divinity is veiled by his humanity. The devil notices these spectacular attributes of Christ and desires to possess him. After Christ's death, the devil thinks he has rights to Christ because he is human, but when Satan bites down on the humanity of Christ (which serves as bait), he is caught by Christ's divinity (the hook that snares the fish). Gregory writes, "In order to secure that the ransom in our behalf might be easily accepted by him who required it [Satan], the Deity was hidden under the veil of our nature, that so, as with ravenous fish, the hook of the Deity might be gulped down along with the bait of the flesh."[30] Because Satan did not have legal rights over the divinity of Christ, he is forced to let him go. Also, because Satan took something that did not belong to him, he must be punished. That punishment is to give up what does belong to him, i.e., humanity. According to this model, Christ offers himself as a ransom paid to redeem all of humanity, and in this way, is victorious over Satan and his powers in freeing humanity for relationship with God.

29. Saint Gregory, "Great Catechism," 492–93.

30. Ibid., 494.

Each of these three sub-theories in the *Christus Victor* category attempts to explain just how Christ achieves victory over the powers of sin, death, and the devil, and they are successful to varying degrees. One of the advantages of the *Christus Victory* category as a whole is that, like the sacrifice model, it connects us to very early Christian ideas and echoes the language of the New Testament. For example, the Gospels of Mark and Matthew describe Jesus as the one who came to give his life as a ransom for many (Mark 10:45; Matt 20:28), while Jesus' words instituting the Eucharist have often been translated as, "This is my blood of the covenant, which is poured out as a ransom for many" (Matt 26:28). Aside from the specific uses of ransom language, the New Testament is full of allusions to Jesus' victory and defeat over the powers of evil, and this metaphor of Christ as victor continues to be familiar and meaningful to contemporary Christians, as demonstrated by the familiarity of the hymns quoted above.

This model also takes seriously the notion that evil is powerful, and that we do seem to be trapped by that power. Paul describes this awareness in his letter to the Romans: "I do not understand my own actions. For I do not do what I want, but the very thing I hate . . . I can will what is right but I cannot do it. For I do not do the good I want, but the evil I do not want is what I do" (Rom 7: 15, 18b–19). Paul describes the personal, individual experience of bondage to evil, but this experience of bondage need not be solely personal and individual. Walter Wink provides a compelling contemporary description of the supreme command that evil has over whole communities and nations: "There is a concentration of evil in a directional pull counter to the will of God. And however intolerable it is when encountered personally, its manifestations are most disastrous when they are social."[31] Whether we experience evil as an individual drive toward disobedience or recognize evil in the structures of oppression in our world, the point remains that evil exists, and the *Christus Victor* model takes that existence seriously.

A final advantage of this model—especially the ransom theory—is that it is logical. While the theory that God sets up this whole series of tricky events to redeem humanity may not seem reasonable to modern

---

31. Wink, *Unmasking the Powers*, 28. Wink's work is especially helpful when trying to understand the *Christus Victor* model in a contemporary framework because he demythologizes (although Wink likely would not use such a word) the spiritual language of the New Testament to show that the evil forces early Christians battled continue to exist in our world; we just call them something different.

Christians, at least the theory explains exactly how God and Christ win victory over evil. The plot line makes sense and answers the pragmatic questions.

Yet despite these advantages, generations of Christians have identified significant problems with this model. First, it makes God out to be a bit of a con artist. Although the whole ransom plan rests on the fact that God is too righteous and just to simply ignore the devil's legal rights and take humanity back, it ends up painting God as a deceitful trickster, and many Christians rejected this picture of God.[32] Such critiques have been present almost from the inception of this model. But this theory has a second disadvantage for contemporary Christians in that a cosmic battle between the forces of good and evil does not make sense in a modern cosmogony. Despite Walter Wink's *Powers* trilogy, which demythologizes the spirit language of the New Testament to make sense in a modern world, most contemporary believers still reject the stark dualism of this model and find its cosmology to be both foreign and irrelevant.[33]

Furthermore, pacifist Christians have rejected the model's military and battle imagery. For those who believe that God is nonviolent and that human salvation rests at least in part on humans following the nonviolent actions of Jesus, this model seems nonsensical. Liberation theology makes a related critique of this model by highlighting the oppression many people face as a result of this identification of Jesus as a victorious king. Throughout history, Christians have often translated the idea of Jesus as the victor to Jesus as the king, a king who implicitly condones and even supports the status quo and those in power. That is, this model

32. In response to criticism that his theory makes God deceitful, Saint Gregory of Nyssa responds that the devil got his just due: "So in this instance, by the reasonable rule of justice, he who had practiced deception receives in turn that very treatment, the seeds of which he had himself sown of his own free will. He who first deceived man by the bait of sensual pleasure is himself deceived by the presentment of the human form" (Saint Gregory, "Great Catechism," 495).

33. Gerald O'Collins points out that perhaps this notion of a cosmic battle is not too far removed from the modern psyche, given the popularity of films such as those in the *Star Wars* series (O'Collins, *Interpreting Jesus*, 144). Clearly modern people are fascinated and entertained by this classic battle between good and evil, but people's willingness to be entertained by the story of this duality is not a justification for advocating a model of atonement that only works on the mythical level. This is because such a model demands that contemporary people continue to think of religion in a mythical worldview that is otherwise quite removed from their everyday lives in the scientific world.

of *Christus Victor* has often re-imagined the Christ in the image of the powerful.[34]

Finally, the question remains whether Christ actually has overcome the powers of evil in this world. A quick glance through the daily newspaper's headlines reveals that murder, poverty, starvation, genocide, torture, and destruction of all kinds are still rampant in our world. This kind of evidence throws doubt on the claim that Christ really has been victorious.

Satisfaction

The *Christus Victor* model and its sub-theories held sway throughout the early centuries of Christian theology. Not until the Middle Ages did a new understanding of atonement grab Christians' attention: the satisfaction theory. Anselm of Canterbury proposed this theory in order to combat the ransom theory and what he viewed as the most glaring weaknesses of that theory: that Satan has legal rights over humanity which God must recognize, and that God would act in a deceitful way. Therefore, Anselm's theory highlights God's justice.

According to Anselm, humanity sins by not giving proper honor to God: "A person who does not render God this honor due Him, takes from God what is His and dishonors God, and this is to commit sin."[35] In other words, sin is not affording to God what is due. In order to overcome or atone for that sin and put humanity back in right relationship to God, humanity must honor God. But that alone is not enough. Because God has been offended by human actions, people must do something extra to offer recompense for the offense. We might think about this something extra as similar to the settlement a jury awards for pain and suffering. It goes above and beyond mere repayment of the debt. Satisfaction, then, according to Anselm, is both of these pieces together: the restoration of honor plus the offering of recompense.

Anselm viewed justice as one of God's most important attributes. Therefore, he reasoned that God could not simply ignore sin, for that would violate God's justice and also deny the weight of sin.[36] God's justice demands that something be done to atone for sin, and Anselm sees

---

34. See, for example, Sobrino, *Jesus the Liberator*, 12–22.

35. Anselm, *Why God Became Man*, 84.

36. Ibid., 85–87.

two possibilities. Either satisfaction must be made, or humanity must be punished. But God is also merciful. Therefore, God decides that instead of inflicting punishment on all of humanity, God will provide the means by which humanity can offer satisfaction.

Humanity is incapable of offering satisfaction for our sins because the satisfaction must be given in measure to the sin. All of the ways that humanity would repay God for sin (such as repentance, a contrite heart, bodily labors, forgiveness of others, obedience, etc.) are what we already owe to God simply for being our creator. There is nothing with which humanity could pay for our sin that we do not already owe to God.[37] Instead, satisfaction must be made by someone greater than human- ity—indeed, greater than everything that exists. Of course, only God can accomplish such a thing. And yet, humans must be the ones to offer satis- faction because it is as compensation for our sin. The only solution to this dilemma, according to Anselm, is that the God-man must make the satis- faction. He writes, "It is needful that the very same Person who is to make this satisfaction be perfect God and perfect man, since no one can do it except one who is truly God, and no one ought to do it except one who is truly man."[38] God must enter into the human race (be born of Adam) in order that the satisfaction may be made by a human.[39] Thus, because Christ offers his own life as repayment and recompense, humanity is not punished, and God's justice (not God's wrath) is satisfied.[40] In this way, Christ's death effects human salvation because he deserves recompense for choosing to give up his life when the divine part of him was under no obligation to do so, but there is no way he can be rewarded because he is already God. Therefore, payment must be made to someone else, and that payment takes the form of human salvation.[41]

Above all else, Anselm strove to make his theory reasonable, and that may be one of its biggest advantages. He believed that faith can be

---

37. Additionally, because all humans are sinful, there is no way that a human could overcome his or her own sin to a degree that he or she would be able to offer compen- sation on behalf of another person. Anselm writes, "Man, the sinner, can by no means do this, because one who is a sinner cannot justify another sinner" (ibid., 69–70).

38. Ibid., 125.

39. Anselm points out that if God had acted in any other way, humanity would be servants of the one who redeemed them, not servants of God (ibid., 69–70).

40. It is important for Anselm that Christ *offered* his life. He was not compelled by God, so this is not a case of divine abuse.

41. Ibid., 160.

reached by clear reasoning and therefore does not have to rely on mythical worldviews and fantastical leaps of faith.[42] For that reason, he tried to show that one could reach his conclusions about the necessity for a God-man quite independent of the Christian faith tradition.

Another advantage of this theory is that it balances God's justice and mercy. The emphasis on God's justice acknowledges that sin is a serious matter, but sin and punishment are not the whole of the story. God goes to great lengths to offer a way for humans to render satisfaction rather than be punished, and this reveals a merciful and creative God.

The satisfaction theory revolves around the concepts of honor and offense, qualities that, while still important in the contemporary world, no longer carry the same importance as they did in the context of Anselm's medieval Europe. During the Middle Ages, the idea that satisfaction was required for pardon was universal; Anselm just applied it to the work of Christ. He also incorporated ideas of medieval chivalry into his theory, such as the necessity of compensation for injured honor.[43] Given that these ideas (especially chivalry) carry less importance in the modern world, the satisfaction theory seems out of step with the worldview of contemporary Christians.

Substitution

Many Christians seem to have conflated the satisfaction theory (sometimes known as propitiation) and the penal substitution (sometimes known as expiation) theory, which may be understandable. [44] Both models involve human atonement for wrongdoing in order to win God's favor, but they differ in their understanding of the purpose of that atoning action. The model of propitiation usually describes an angry God who must be placated by the blood of an innocent victim before overlooking the

---

42. Ibid., 67.

43. Foley, *Anselm's Theory of Atonement*, 107, 113.

44. As Schmiechen points out, this tendency is probably due to Gustav Aulén's influence. In his *Christus Victor*, he groups the major theories of atonement into just three categories: *Christus Victor*, satisfaction, and moral influence. Because penal substitution fits most closely with the satisfaction theory in that Christ's death acts as a sort of transaction that changes God, he lumps penal substitution into the satisfaction category. As a result, all of the critiques of penal substitution are lobbed against satisfaction when those criticisms may not equally apply to satisfaction (Schmiechen, *Saving Power*, 196).

wrongdoings of sinners, whereas expiation emphasizes an amendment for sin. Propitiation is more focused on God and on appeasing God's wrath, whereas expiation is more concerned with how humans must atone for their sins.[45] In this way, the two theories are quite different. Whereas Anselm's theory focused on God's justice, the penal substitution theory depends on legal justice. Also, Anselm practically bends over backwards to show that God does not want to punish humanity for sin, but later theologians did not have the same qualms about a vengeful and angry God. Hints of the penal substitution theory can be detected in the theologies of Martin Luther and even more clearly in John Calvin, but the fullest expression of the theory comes from Charles Hodge, a nineteenth-century Reformed systematic theologian who had a long and influential teaching career at Princeton Theological Seminary.

Penal substitution theory is quite simple and probably the most familiar of all of these atonement models to contemporary American readers. In fact, it seems that a large portion of contemporary Christians not only believe that penal substitution is the best explanation of Jesus' death and our salvation, but that it is the *only* valid explanation.[46]

According to the penal substitution model, humans sin by disobeying God's law, which incurs God's wrath and separates us from God. Hodge explains the problem like this: "The first and most obvious consequence of sin, is subjection to the penalty of the law. The wages of sin is death. Every sin of necessity subjects the sinner to the wrath and curse of God."[47] Then, relying on legal metaphors, the theory explains that all of humanity is judged guilty before God and so stands under the penalty of death.[48] All of humanity must be punished, but because God is merciful, God sends Christ to stand in our stead and receive our punishment.[49] Thus, Jesus stands in as the victim of God's wrath, receives our punishment, appeases God's anger such that God "acquits" humanity, and thus

---

45. McIntyre, *Shape of Soteriology*, 35–39.

46. Green and Baker, *Recovering the Scandal*, 13.

47. Hodge, *Systematic Theology*, 516.

48. Ibid., 482–83, 485.

49. Hodge goes on to contrast the guiltiness of humans and Jesus' innocence as our substitute: "Men can be pardoned and restored to the favour of God, because Christ was set forth as an expiation for their sins, through faith in his blood because He was made a curse for us; because He died, the just for the unjust; because He bore our sins in his own body on the tree and because the penalty due to us was laid on him" (Hodge, *Systematic Theology*, 492).

restores the relationship between God and humanity.[50] This model contrasts human guilt against Christ's innocence such that humanity must recognize the great gift that Christ has given us. We are to be exceedingly grateful that as our substitute, Christ took on the horrific punishment meant for us. As such, one of the hallmarks of this theory is its emphasis on the great suffering Christ endured through his passion.[51]

Perhaps this theory's simplicity is what has made this model popular for generations of Christians. Another advantage is that the theory simultaneously maintains God's justice and mercy. The justice here is of the retributive kind, meaning that people get what they deserve, which might seem comforting to some. If God did not operate out of this kind of justice, perhaps the world would feel even more chaotic.

Despite the popularity of this model, critiques of it are numerous, and they come from multiple locations within the Christian community. Feminist, womanist, and black theologians have reacted to the way this theory celebrates Jesus' role as victim and valorizes his suffering,[52] while several Anabaptist scholars have rejected the violence inherent in this theory as well as the way the theory separates atonement and ethics.[53] Indeed, Hodge writes that the suffering and death that Jesus endured "were divine inflictions. It pleased the Lord to bruise Him [Jesus]."[54] Clearly, this notion that God enjoys acting violently denies the Anabaptist theological norm that God is nonviolent.

Finally, voices from both the Anabaptist and Pietist traditions critique this model because it requires nothing from the believer. As discussed earlier, both of these traditions emphasize that Christians are called to live out their faith and their salvation through lives of discipleship, and

---

50. John Calvin writes, "Our acquittal is in this—that the guilt which made us liable to punishment was transferred to the head of the Son of God . . . Christ, in his death, was offered to the Father as a propitiatory victim" (Calvin, *Institutes of the Christian Religion*, 327–29).

51. Indeed, this is most likely the reason that the recent film, *The Passion of the Christ*, shows Jesus' suffering in such great detail. See Gibson et al., *The Passion of the Christ*.

52. See, for example, Brown and Parker, "For God So Loved the World?"; Brock and Parker, *Proverbs of Ashes*; Cone, *God of the Oppressed*; and Williams, *Sisters in the Wilderness*.

53. While there are certainly other critiques of this theory, a full discussion of the many problems with this theory falls outside the scope of this study and has been taken up further by many excellent books.

54. Hodge, *Systematic Theology*, 517.

yet the penal substitution model is completely objective. God and Jesus work out the details of the salvific plan without any actions on the part of the believer. For this reason, Martin Luther can urge his friend to "be a sinner and sin boldly"[55] because neither repentance nor discipleship is required for salvation in this model.

Valorization of Suffering

Feminist and womanist theologians have critiqued the penal substitution theory because it claims that suffering is redemptive. It argues that Jesus' suffering is good and necessary for the salvation of all people, and these scholars note that this is just a hop, skip, and a jump away from the assertion that because it was good that Jesus suffered, it is good that we suffer as well. Self-sacrifice and obedience then become the very definition of a faithful Christian.[56] This is especially problematic for feminists and womanists because women are often on the underside of power relationships, and as a result, experience suffering. These scholars argue that to tell women to remain in their situations of oppression in order to be like Jesus and win Jesus' reward is appalling. Pastor and theologian Rebecca Parker tells a horrific story of a parishioner who was abused by her husband and resolved to stay in the relationship because of the theology she had heard her whole life that rested on the penal substitution theory. Recounting this woman's reasoning for staying in such an abusive situation, Parker writes, "A good woman would be willing to accept personal pain, and think only of the good of the family. You know, 'Your life is only valuable if it's given away' and 'This is your cross to bear.' She heard . . . that Jesus didn't turn away from the cup of suffering when God asked him to drink it. She was trying to be a good Christian, to follow in the footsteps of Jesus."[57] The tragic ending to Parker's story is that the woman embraced this traditional Christian reasoning, returned to her husband, and was murdered by him. Thus, although the penal substation model did not kill this woman, the theology it influences can clearly be harmful.

Womanist theologian Delores Williams argues that the model of Jesus as suffering substitute or surrogate is especially problematic for African American women, given their history of forced surrogacy. She

55. Luther, "Let Your Sins Be Strong," para. 13.

56. Brown and Parker, "For God So Loved the World?" 2.

57. Brock and Parker, *Proverbs of Ashes*, 18.

writes that black women cannot glorify the cross because to do so "is to glorify suffering and to render their [own] exploitation sacred. To do so is to glorify the sin of defilement."[58]

Central to both of these critiques (and others like them[59]) is the fact that the penal substitution model emphasizes that Jesus' suffering is innocent and undeserved, that this innocent suffering is the means by which salvation is achieved, that this innocent suffering reveals God's (and Jesus') love for us, and that if we are loving towards our fellow human and towards God, we too will embrace undeserved suffering. In fact, many sermons teach that this is the heart of the Christian message and the heart of what it means to be a Christian.[60]

A closely related critique of this model is that it paints God as a horrible monster, perhaps even as a divine child abuser, for it depicts "God the father demanding and carrying out the suffering and death of his own son."[61] On the other hand, God appears as an enraged man who cannot control his anger and must lash out. This anthropomorphism is destructive in two particular ways. First, it legitimizes this emotional response in humans: Of course it is reasonable to lose control of one's temper and strike out at someone; even God does it! Second, it limits God's creativity and imagination to assume that God reacts in anger like a human person would.

Anabaptist and Pietist Critiques of Penal Substitution

Although Anabaptists are certainly not the only ones to react negatively to the violence inherent in this model, they are well suited to make this critique because there is much in this model that conflicts with the particular emphases of traditional Anabaptist theology. First, contemporary Anabaptist scholars reject the notion that God redeems all of humanity through a violent act.[62] To claim that God desires the death of anyone, let alone an innocent victim, violates an Anabaptist theological norm—that

58. Williams, *Sisters in the Wilderness*, 167.

59. Gregory Love provides an excellent summary of many critiques of an abusive love in chapter 2 of his *Love, Violence, and the Cross*, 27–51.

60. See, for example, King, "Suffering and Faith," 41–42.

61. Brown and Parker, "For God So Loved the World?" 9.

62. Peter Abelard makes the same critique, arguing that God should be more angered by humanity's heinous killing of Christ than by Adam's slight transgression (Abelard, *Epistle to the Romans*, 166–67).

God is nonviolent. For example, Denny Weaver finds that nonviolence is intrinsic to the teaching, life, and work of Jesus, and therefore intrinsic to the character of God.[63]

Second, this model separates atonement from ethics and discipleship. It does not require much of anything on the part of the believer, and it completely ignores Jesus' life and ministry. According to this model, "Jesus' teachings, moral example, and works of compassion and power were not central to his mission. The death was the apex of the Messiah's work, not its untimely end. Indeed . . . his life's mission was accomplished in the last six hours."[64]

Given the brief sketch of historical Anabaptist theology in chapter one, it should be clear that this model would be problematic for many contemporary Anabaptists and Pietists as well. One of the most important features of Anabaptist soteriology is its insistence that salvation cannot be separated from ethics or discipleship modeled after Jesus' own life. The work of Christ and the ethical demands of being a Christian are integrally linked. Although early Anabaptists used the language of satisfaction theory of atonement, they almost always added that salvation must be lived; an inner transformation must be expressed in outward life. Indeed, an anonymous Anabaptist author (perhaps Michael Sattler) wrote that Christ's satisfaction is efficacious only for those who live the Christian life.[65] Menno Simons echoes this sentiment (though he also incorporates metaphors from the penal substitution model): "It will avail us nothing to be called Christians and boast of the Lord's blood, merits, grace, and gospel, as long as we are not converted from a sinful life. It is all in vain that we are called Christians or that Christ died . . . if we walk

63. Weaver, "Peace-Shaped Theology," 25. Though this claim was widely accepted among historical Anabaptists, contemporary Anabaptist scholars diverge in their opinions. Scott Holland and James Reimer argue that God may have a wrathful, judgmental, and even violent side that cannot be tamed by the politics and example of Jesus. In fact, Holland argues that it is precisely the violence of God that transforms human aggressive energies into nonviolent expressions of peacemaking on earth. See Holland, "Gospel of Peace," 42; and Reimer, *Mennonites and Classical Theology*, 489–92. In general, Anabaptist and Brethren traditions have viewed God through the lens of Jesus' Sermon on the Mount. For that reason, they have tended to disregard the wrathful and violent depictions of God in the Hebrew Bible. Perhaps this one-sided view of God raises the question of whether Brethren are necessarily Marcionites, which, while significant, is beyond the scope of the current study.

64. Love, *Love, Violence, and the Cross*, 11.

65. Friedmann, *Theology of Anabaptism*, 84.

not in obedience to all the commandments of God . . ."[66] Similarly, he argues that there is no word in the Bible that says we are saved without repentance and regeneration simply because we "boast of faith and the death of Christ."[67]

This close connection between faith and works was a hallmark of the early Brethren as well. In the first major statement of Brethren beliefs, Alexander Mack wrote, "Whoever believes in Him [Christ] is justified. Faith in Christ produces obedience and submission to all of His word and commandments."[68] Likewise, Peter Nead, a nineteenth-century Dunker, was suspicious of theologies that suggested salvation is achieved by faith alone (as the penal substitution model implies) and later argued that the rites of the church and the literal obedience of Jesus' teachings were necessary for salvation.[69] Clearly, the early Anabaptists and Brethren were adamant that humanity must participate in salvation, and as such, many contemporary Brethren and Anabaptists reject the penal substitution model.

Moral Exemplar

The last major atonement model we will discuss here was proposed by medieval French theologian Peter Abelard, who was a contemporary of Anselm. He agreed with Anselm that Satan does not hold lawful or rightful power over humanity; however, Abelard objected to the idea that Christ was incarnated in order to offer satisfaction to God. He argued that God does not need to be reconciled to humanity, but rather that humanity must be reconciled to God. In other words, the change effected by atonement or salvation must take place in humanity, not in God. Sin alienates humanity from God and disrupts our integrity; it does not alienate God from humanity. He also rejected the idea that the death of the Son should reconcile humans to God. Instead, he proposed that God's nature as love mandates that God act in order to save sinners. In this

66. Simons, *Foundation and Plain Instruction*, 22.

67. Ibid., 258.

68. Mack, "Basic Questions," 27.

69. Kostlevy, Introduction to *Theological Writings*, v. Nead writes, "Faith is one of the means appointed for salvation, not that faith is salvation, [but] it is only a means appointed. And it is not the only means appointed; there are other means which follow faith and must be observed as well as faith, or we can have no promise of salvation in the New Testament" (Nead, *Theological Writings*, 313).

way, God is motivated by love rather than justice. Christ reveals God's love to humanity, and in Christ, God takes on human nature and teaches humans by word and example, thereby binding humanity to God more fully in love. Christ's laying down his life for sinners is a manifestation of God's love that causes a spiritual transformation in the lives of humans. Thus, Christ reveals God's love to us because nothing exhibits the extent of love like dying for another. [70]

Abelard pointed out that humanity has done nothing to merit the receipt of this love, and it is only after receiving the gift of creative love that we respond by living out lives of true charity. In this way, Christ is an exemplar of the sacrificial love that Christians are to imitate, but this exemplary quality is a secondary consequence of its redeeming quality. Humanity's responsive act of love is a direct result of Christ's transformation of the sinner's person. For Abelard, the manifestation of God's love in Jesus' sacrificial death causes a spiritual transformation in the life of the recipient. It joins the believer to God and neighbor in a bond of affection. In Abelard's own words, "through this matchless grace shown to us that his Son received our nature, and in that nature, teaching us both by word and by example, persevered to the death and bound us to himself even more through love, so that when we have been kindled by so great a benefit of divine grace, true charity might fear to endure nothing for his sake."[71]

For Abelard, the disclosure of divine love is salvation. The manifestation of divine love causes a spiritual transformation within humanity and inspires us to follow Christ's example. Thereby, the bond of love between God and humanity is restored. Divine love is infused in the hearts of sinners and instills a new motive for action. Humanity is freed from slavery to sin and granted new liberty as adopted children of God.

The moral influence model is quite different from the other models we have examined, and perhaps that is its first advantage. In the first place, it highlights the fact that God's motivation in providing atonement is love, not justice, anger, or offense. Second, it values Jesus' life and ministry and does not view the whole purpose of the incarnation to be Jesus' death. Given that so much Anabaptist and Brethren theology and ethics

---

70. Abelard, *Epistle to the Romans*, 168.

71. Ibid., 167–68.

rests on Jesus' lived example, the fact that this model takes that example into account is surely one of its strengths.

Another strength is that this model recognizes that the problem of alienation and separation lies with humanity, not with God. It requires a change in us rather than some hocus pocus that makes God view us differently. As such, it necessitates human action. We must actually do something in order to mend our relationship with God rather than sit passively by while God and Christ work out our salvation. Because this model demands a human response and action, it is known as a subjective theory of atonement. Humanity is the subject or agent of the action that leads to salvation. When we claim that agency and become more loving, that change in attitude mends our relationship with God. In contrast, all the other theories discussed in this chapter are objective theories. Under objective theories of atonement, humans are the objects of the activities that God or Christ do on our behalf, and those activities accomplish atonement for all people for all time. According to these theories, God and Christ have worked out some kind of arrangement (often outside of human history) such that humans do not have to do anything. We simply accept that salvation has already occurred and that it has occurred for everyone, for these theories view humanity as an ontological category rather than as individuals who carry out individual actions. However, as a subjective theory, the moral influence model provides for individual atonement. Under this model, salvation is not an act of divine tyranny. Rather, there is some human responsibility or acceptance, for only those who take the necessary action—those who witness and respond to Jesus' actions—appropriate atonement. In this way, the moral influence theory brings atonement and discipleship back together, and as such, is more in line with Anabaptist and Brethren views of salvation.

Of all the theories discussed in this chapter, the moral influence theory is probably the one that feels most comfortable for many Brethren. However, there remains an important problem with this model: it does not explain why Jesus died. The notion that Jesus laid down his life for others so that they may understand the extent of God's love for them may be a beautiful idea, but if salvation is the disclosure of divine love, why is such a death necessary? The moral influence theory does not answer this question, and so our search for a meaningful way to understand atonement and salvation that aligns with Anabaptist theology cannot end with any of the historical models of atonement discussed here. In the next chapter, we turn to more contemporary models drawn from many different Christian traditions.

CHAPTER 3

Contemporary Models of Atonement

As the last chapter demonstrated, Christian theology has not worked out once and for all exactly how Jesus' life, death, and resurrection cause salvation. Multiple theories have gained and lost popularity, depending on how closely each theory corresponded to the worldview of a given place and time. Because humans' worldview continues to change, theologians continue to propose new theories. Numerous theories have been proposed just within the last half-century, and we will examine just a small sampling of these theories to get a feeling for the ideas and themes contemporary theologians think are important for this day and age.[1] I have chosen models that have resonance with the particular Anabaptist themes we highlighted in the earlier chapters and that offer some ideas that may appeal to a contemporary Brethren view. Most of the models we consider in this chapter come from the late twentieth century, but we begin with an earlier atonement model proposed by Walter Rauschenbusch.

Walter Rauschenbusch

Walter Rauschenbusch is considered the spokesperson for the Social Gospel movement, which was a sect within American Protestant Christianity in the early part of the twentieth century. Rauschenbusch was clearly influenced by his own social context. He lived during America's

---

1. Jersak and Hardin's book *Stricken by God?* offers a wonderful collection of essays that propose nonviolent atonement models. Some of those models will be examined in the following chapter, so we need not repeat the work of that book here.

so-called Gilded Age and watched the growing chasm between the super-rich robber barons and those who suffered horrible conditions working in these barons' factories, including those forced into child labor. He saw that the Protestant churches of his time emphasized individual re-generation and heavenly salvation instead of addressing the concerns of people living in the real world. He worried that Christianity would become irrelevant and meaningless if it continued to promise future bliss while overlooking the present social crisis on Earth. Rauschenbusch and those in the Social Gospel movement were concerned about the social injustices of their world and determined that Christianity should address such injustice. They believed that the purpose of Christianity is not sim-ply a matter of believing the right things and waiting until heaven for suffering and injustice to end. They were sure that ethics play a crucial role in Christianity and that being a good Christian meant engaging the world in a way that improves the lives of others. Therefore, participants in this movement brought their Christian ethics to bear on issues such as poverty, child labor, alcoholism, homelessness, and many other social ills, believing that Jesus delivered a mandate to his followers to care for "the least of these" (Matt 25:31–46). But what separated this Christian movement from others concerned with ethics was that they engaged the systems of the world to bring about positive changes for society rather than just for individuals. Rather than simply providing meals or praying for a family mired in poverty, adherents to the Social Gospel movement worked with labor unions to improve wages and conditions for working people, believing that Christians are called to be active in the world on behalf of others.

Given this background to the movement, it should not be surprising that Rauschenbusch's understanding of atonement fits quite closely with the moral exemplar theory. Rauschenbusch picked up Abelard's idea that an inward transformation leads to an outward change of life. This change produces new hope, courage, and insight, along with new warmth of love and strength of will, all of which lead to a desire to help others. Without this change, we continue to exist in a state of sin, which Rauschenbusch defined as selfishness and self-centeredness, or putting one's own profit and ambitions above the welfare of others. If this self-centeredness is sin, then salvation is a change that turns a person away from the self and to-ward God and humanity.[2] This change is precisely that which is wrought by an experience of God's love as manifested in the life and death of Jesus.

2. Rauschenbusch, *Theology for the Social Gospel*, 97.

In this way, Rauschenbusch's theory is quite similar to Abelard's. But what separates the two models is Rauschenbusch's social dimension—both of sin and salvation.

For Rauschenbusch, sin is not just individual selfishness or a "private transaction between the sinner and God."[3] Instead, sin has communal implications; it is super-personal in that it affects the whole of society rather than just isolated individuals. Therefore, salvation must also go beyond the individual. In this way, this Social Gospel atonement model addresses one of the critiques of the moral exemplar theory, namely that it is too individualistic.

First, Rauschenbusch explains the social or communal nature of sin. He argues that Jesus was affected by sin, but not by the sins of a few individuals. Instead, Jesus endured and was eventually killed by six specific social sins.[4] The first of these sins is religious bigotry. Rauschenbusch explains that Jesus was killed by leaders of Judaism who thought he was trying to overthrow their religion, and thus, their power.[5] The combination of greed and political power is the second social sin Jesus withstood. The ruling religious classes thought Jesus was trying to stir up revolutionary elements that would cause them to lose their power. Third, Jesus experienced the corruption of justice in a court system (like those of Rauschenbusch's own day) that treated the wealthy and poor unequally. Rauschenbusch writes, "So Jesus made experience of one of the permanent sins of organized society, bearing in his own body and soul what so many thousands of the poor and weak have borne before and after, the corruption of justice."[6] Fourth, Jesus was the victim of mob spirit and action, perhaps the best example of social sin. Individuals may be able to maintain self-control, but when the mob mentality takes hold, the group loses control and ends up perpetrating crimes the individual would never consider committing. Fifth, Jesus suffered the effects of militarism.

---

3. Ibid., 48.

4. See ibid., 249–58.

5. Rauschenbusch writes, "He was suspected of far-reaching designs against the religion of Jehovah; he had offered to substitute a temple not made with hands for their ancestral sanctuary . . . Religious bigotry has been one of the permanent evils of mankind, the cause of untold social division, bitterness, persecution, and religious wars. It is always a social sin. Estimate the harm which the exponents of religion have done simply by suppressing the prophetic minds who had received from God fresh thought on spiritual and intellectual problems, and by cowing those who might have followed the prophets" (ibid., 249–50).

6. Ibid., 252–54.

Rauschenbusch points out that Jesus never participated in a war himself, but he did fall into the war system after his arrest. He suffered from the treatment of the soldiers who were themselves affected by the war system. Finally, the last social sin Jesus endured was class contempt, which Rauschenbusch argues is the "direct negation of solidarity and love."[7] In fact, Rauschenbusch saved his harshest critique for this almost universal social sin, calling it "a sinful denial of the kingdom of God, and one of the characteristic marks and forces of the Kingdom of Evil."[8] Crucifixion was a punishment reserved for the lowest classes in Roman society, and as Rauschenbusch explains, "When Jesus was nailed to the tree, therefore, he bore not only the lightning shoots of physical pain imposed by the cruelties of criminal law, but also the contempt for the lower classes which has always dehumanized the upper classes, numbed and crippled the spiritual self-respect of the lower classes, and set up insuperable barriers to the spirit of the kingdom of God."[9] Rauschenbusch details Jesus' suffering through these six social sins in order to show that it was not just the actions of a few individuals that killed Jesus. Instead, Jesus died as a result of the systems of power that serve to elevate some at the expense of the many, systems that Rauschenbusch calls "the Kingdom of Evil."

Rauschenbusch argues that we participate in this Kingdom of Evil by perpetuating the social sins that killed Jesus: "We are linked in a solidarity of evil and guilt with all who have done the same before us, and all who will do the same after us. In so far then as we, by our conscious sanctions or our passive consent, have repeated the sins which killed Jesus, we have made ourselves guilty of his death."[10] As long as we live and participate in this Kingdom of Evil, we are out of union and fellowship with God. Christ was the first to fully live in consciousness of God by sharing God's will, which he acted out through his life and ministry. He drew others into his realization of God so that others appropriated God's will for others as their own. In this way, Jesus initiated a new spiritual life, and humanity was lifted to a new level of spiritual existence. This new spiritual existence provokes a new "cooperative unity of will"[11] between God and humans. In other words, humans now follow God's desires

7. Ibid., 256.

8. Ibid.

9. Ibid., 257.

10. Ibid., 259.

11. Ibid., 265.

for others rather than falling back into self-centered concern for personal power. Therefore, the work of Christ is to draw people into greater God-consciousness.

Like Abelard, Rauschenbusch rejected the idea that Christ's death changed God's relation to humanity and affirmed that Christ's life was more important than his death. This transformation, which brings about salvation, does not come about through "a legal transaction but by the presence of a new and decisive factor embodied in the racial life which affected its spiritual value and potency."[12] In other words, witnessing Jesus' example of a life devoted to God produces the change in humanity that leads to reconciliation between humans' will (concern for self) and God's will (concern for others). This reconciliation was not conditional on his death; in fact, his life and ministry could have continued for another thirty years.

But Rauschenbusch did find some value in Christ's death, and the benefits are two-fold: it indicts all of humanity for our participation in social sin, and it spreads the message of Jesus' life in a highly effective way. First, Jesus' death reveals our own guilt for participation in social sin. When humans hear the story of Christ's suffering and death, we should recognize our own complicity in these social sins, which continue today. While his death may not be the cause of our salvation, it is necessary in that it makes us aware of the need for salvation. Rauschenbusch writes, "In so far as a genuine consciousness of sin is the first step toward redemption from sin, the cross was an essential part of the redemptive process."[13] But second, "The life of Christ never spread such a realization of sin as his death has done."[14] Therefore, in Rauschenbusch's model, Jesus' death is necessary, though not because God willed it. It is necessary merely because it was an effective way for people to witness Jesus' devotion to God's will.

Just as sin has a social dimension in Rauschenbusch's model, so too does salvation. Rauschenbusch worried that traditional theology had no doctrine of *social* redemption. Rauschenbusch differed from many traditional theologians in that he believed salvation necessarily has a corporate element that must be realized in this world. He viewed salvation as all of society (corporations, institutions, economic systems, etc.) coming

12. Ibid.

13. Ibid., 270.

14. Ibid.

under the law of Christ. Rauschenbusch called this the Christianizing of the social order, and he defined it as bringing the social order into harmony with the ethical convictions we identify with Christ.[15] The role of Christians in this model of salvation is to follow Christ's example in relating to others. The mature Christian should pattern his or her life as closely as possible on that of Christ: "True Christian regeneration results in an outlook toward humanity and an interest in a higher social consciousness. The realization of social solidarity is one of the distinctive marks of a true follower of Jesus."[16] In other words, when Christians witness the love of God manifested in Jesus' way of life, they realize that salvation is not so much a matter of heaven as it is of social solidarity. Full salvation is the changing of humanity, society, and the environment for the betterment of all. Salvation does not just change individuals, or even just society; it also includes super-personal forces—those groups, organizations, institutions, communities, etc., that are so bound up that they think, act, and sin as one. For salvation to be realized, these forces too must be converted so that they better serve the good of all rather than exploiting the many for the benefit of a few.

Whereas much of Rauschenbusch's model is dependent on Abelard's theory of atonement, his model of social salvation could be likened to a demythologized version of the *Christus Victor* model. Rauschenbusch agreed that there are forces of evil in the world that pull on humanity, and he identified these super-personal forces as groups, organizations, and institutions that manipulate people and things for their own selfish ends. These super-personal forces exert various kinds of authority over us and greatly influence our corporate life.

However, the similarity between Rauschenbusch's and the *Christus Victor* models stops there. Whereas the *Christus Victor* model suggests that this cosmic drama between good and evil happens outside of history (even though it argues that Christ actually entered into human misery), Rauschenbusch maintained a much more this-worldly focus. His social gospel was largely confined to humanity and the earth, not supernatural (not to be confused with super-personal) powers. For Rauschenbusch, salvation and regeneration does not include just the triumph over evil forces, but also a higher social consciousness. It involves changing people, societies, and the environment.

15. Cecil, "Rauschenbusch's Concept of Man," 26. See also Rauschenbusch, *Christianizing the Social Order.*

16. Ibid., *Theology for the Social Gospel,* 108–109.

Another difference between the two models is that whereas *Christus Victor* is completely objective, Rauschenbusch's theory is mostly subjective. According to Rauschenbusch, salvation and sanctification must include an ethical component. This includes submitting to the supremacy of the common good. In the *Christus Victor* model, humans are in bondage to evil in the form of the devil and can only be freed by Christ's victory, but Rauschenbusch argued that contact with Jesus (found in the church as the community that carries the memory of his life) can so strengthen the God-consciousness in us that we are able the overcome the power of sin and rise to newness of life.[17]

Rauschenbusch extracted what he felt to be the most compelling elements of the *Christus Victor* theory and the moral exemplar theory and combined them into a model that made sense in his own early twentieth-century American context. Though our own contemporary context differs sharply from the early twentieth century in some regards, some important consistencies remain, and so Rauschenbusch's model has much to offer contemporary Brethren believers. First, his model draws heavily on Jesus' example, as does much traditional Anabaptist theology. For Rauschenbusch, as for many contemporary Brethren, Jesus' life and ministry is the heart of Christianity, not his death. Second, though he does not use these words, Rauschenbusch's model demands a life of discipleship from Christian believers.[18] The whole point of atonement for Rauschenbusch is to effect positive change in people's lives and society. This can only happen as a result of people following Jesus' example.

Despite these important points of contact between Rauschenbusch's model and traditional Anabaptist theology, there remains a glaring divergence. That social forces must be changed such that all of society can be redeemed is one of the best aspects of Rauschenbusch's model, but when he argues that salvation is the Christianizing of the social order, Brethren grow wary. Many Anabaptists (both historical and contemporary) identify Emperor Constantine's conversion as the point at which Christianity went awry. Anabaptists call the elevation of Christianity to the religion of the empire "the Constantinian shift" or "Constantinianism," which they define as the marriage of church and society under the patronage

---

17. Ibid., 125.

18. Rauschenbusch talks about ethics in terms of bringing about the kingdom of God. He laments the fact that Christianity has lost Jesus' emphasis on the kingdom and focuses instead on doctrine, dogma, and worship (ibid., 131–45).

of political authority.[19] The Constantinian shift switched Christianity from its position as the persecuted minority to a position of status and power. As the church acquired power, it began to have a vested interest in maintaining the status quo. It therefore became more reticent in critiquing the state. Mennonite theologian John Howard Yoder writes, "If, as the New Testament indicates, . . . God calls his people to a prophetically critical relationship to the structures of power and oppression, then the alliance between Rome-as-Empire and Church-as-Hierarchy, which the fourth and fifth centuries gradually consolidated, is not merely a possible tactical error but a structural denial of the gospel."[20] Because the Constantinian church is intimately involved in those structures of power and oppression, it loses the capacity and necessary distance to be critical. The church's involvement in those power structures also has the effect of blessing them, and so it is not too long before the marriage of church and empire leads the evils of the empire (including those six social sins Jesus endured) to become a part of the church. For this reason, Anabaptists have long insisted on a separation between the church and the world that does not allow for the Christianizing of the social order that Rauschenbusch prescribed.[21]

Jürgen Moltmann

There are important points of contact between Rauschenbusch's atonement model and Moltmann's understanding of atonement. Both have a keen interest in this world and refuse to relegate the whole of salvation to some after-death reward. However, how they view God at work in the world differs dramatically. Each of these men's contexts plays an important role in their understandings of atonement. Although Rauschenbusch witnessed poverty and suffering in his New York congregation, he lived during a period of the twentieth century that was fairly optimistic about humanity and human potential. It makes sense, then, that Rauschenbusch's atonement model is also optimistic, stressing what humanity can do rather than the awful state of sin in which we all languish. Moltmann,

19. Heilke, "Yoder's Idea of Constantinianism," 92.

20. Yoder, *Priestly Kingdom*, 245.

21. This is not to say, however, that the strict separation of church and the world is always a good thing within Anabaptist theology and ecclesiology. Indeed, I argue that this Anabaptist insistence on separation from the world has unintentionally hindered Anabaptist relief work around the world (Eisenbise, *For Thy Neighbors' Good*).

on the other hand, lived in Germany through the Second World War. He witnessed the extreme suffering that resulted from Hitler's attempt to Christianize the social order. For that reason, Moltmann's theory differs from Rauschenbusch's model in two important ways. First, rather than advocating that Christians work to build the kingdom of God, Moltmann stresses that establishing God's reign on Earth is God's work. Second, rather than stressing the goodness of humanity and our capacity to do good, Moltmann emphasizes the empathetic suffering of God. In general, Moltmann takes sin and suffering more seriously than does Rauschenbusch.

To begin, Moltmann rejects the Greek metaphysical axiom that God stands apart from this world, impassible, unmovable, and self-sufficing in favor of the biblical picture of "a God full of passion for the life of his people and for justice on his earth"[22] who therefore can really love creation.[23] Rather than starting with the traditional question of how Jesus' death on the cross redeems us, Moltmann begins with the question of what the cross of Jesus means for God's own self.[24] And his answer is that in the death of Jesus, God experiences true grief. Therefore, regardless of whatever else happens on the cross (i.e., how it affects humanity), this event is first and foremost an experience of and between God and Jesus. This event affects God in profound ways, and only because of that fact does it have an effect on humanity. Moltmann writes, "It is the unconditioned and therefore boundless love which proceeds from the grief of the Father and the dying of the Son and reaches forsaken men in order to create in them the possibility and the force of new life."[25] According to Moltmann, then, salvation is precipitated by God's suffering because in God's experience, all suffering is taken up into God. Because of this fact, "there is no suffering which in this history of God is not God's suffering; no death which has not been God's death in the history of Golgotha."[26] And once we become aware of God's love and presence in our suffering,

22. Moltmann, "Crucified God: Yesterday and Today," 130.

23. Moltmann writes, "a God who cannot suffer is poorer than any man. For a God who is incapable of suffering is a being who cannot be involved. Suffering and injustice do not affect him. And because he is so completely insensitive, he cannot be affected or shaken by anything. He cannot weep, for he has no tears. But the one who cannot suffer cannot love either" (ibid., 222).

24. Ibid., *Crucified God*, 201.

25. Ibid., 245.

26. Ibid., 246.

we experience the true nature of God as love. Being loved in this way opens up new freedoms and possibilities for humanity, and it takes us into the inner life of God.

Moltmann points out that living in the love of God in this way puts people at odds with the world because it liberates us from social norms and idolatrous social images. He writes, "Just as the unconditional love of Jesus for the rejected made the Pharisees his enemies and brought him to the cross, so unconditional love also means enmity and persecution in a world in which the life of man is made dependent on particular social norms, conditions, and achievements. A love which takes precedence and robs these conditions of their force is folly and scandal in this world."[27] In other words, experiencing and reciprocating the suffering love of God produces a change in us that puts us in conflict with the ways of the world. Therefore, our present experience is colored by suffering, evil, and death, but according to Moltmann, God is with us in that experience and is transforming us through divine love and compassion. He argues that the Christian hope is that what will be—the world to come—is different from the present reality, and Christians are called to live into that hope by leaving behind the God-forsaken ways of the world. But that world to come is not in some heaven after death. Rather, Christian hope in the eschatological kingdom of God "can have nothing to do with fleeing the world, with resignation and with escapism. In this hope the soul does not soar above our vale of tears to some imagined heavenly bliss, nor does it sever itself from the earth."[28] Instead, it is the hope for and faith in a different kind of world that causes Christians to resist the current ways of the world. Indeed, "those who hope in Christ can no longer put up with reality as it is, but begin to suffer under it, to contradict it. Peace with God means conflict with the world, for the goad of the promised future stabs inexorably into the flesh of every unfulfilled present."[29] In this way, Moltmann's model includes a role for the believer. Christians are the ones who live into this future reality by breaking out of their socially fixed roles. He argues, "If the God who called them to life should expect of them something other than what modern industrial society expects and requires of them, then Christians must venture an exodus and regard their social roles as a new Babylonian exile."[30] We must not blindly adapt

27. Ibid., 248.
28. Ibid., *Theology of Hope*, 21.
29. Ibid.
30. Ibid., 324.

to social structures that do not correspond to the better future God will bring. We must "resist the institutional stabilizing of things,"[31] meaning that we are to resist the status quo and instead push the world toward new and creative options that are more in line with our eschatological hope.

Because salvation is not (solely) a matter of an after-death reward, and because Christians have a responsibility to care for the world by urging it on to better ways, Moltmann's model contains an element of communal or social salvation. In fact, he argues that one of the most important tasks of Christianity is to break out of its socially assigned task of the "saving and preserving of personal, individual, and private humanity."[32] That is, if it does not actually work to change the social conditions of the world, faith becomes irrelevant.

The fact that Moltmann's theory contains a concrete role for the believer connects nicely with traditional Anabaptist theology, but perhaps his emphasis is slightly different than theirs was. Moltmann seems to suggest that the life of action in the world is an inevitable consequence of the eschatological hope that comes from faith and the experience of knowing God in one's own suffering. In this way, perhaps his ideas stand closer to those of the Protestant Reformers who believed grace and salvation come first, and that a life of discipleship comes as a result of that faith. The earliest Anabaptists stressed that a life of obedience does not follow *from* salvation but instead is necessary, along with faith, *for* salvation. Despite this difference, Moltmann's theory of atonement corrects the deficiency of many of the traditional models in which atonement happens completely outside of human history and humanity has nothing to do with it. Moltmann certainly puts God back into history (or better yet, puts all of history into God) by presenting a model that cares deeply for all of creation in its current state of imperfection.

Moltmann's theory also improves on traditional models' understanding of God as one who is not only removed from the world, but is completely unaffected by it. Other models affirm that God loves humanity, which is why God brings about salvation, but Moltmann's point that a God who cannot be affected cannot really love is well taken. Surely a God who suffers cares more deeply for creation than a God who is completely removed. It seems too that the God who suffers will be even more motivated to end the suffering that humanity endures. Perhaps Moltmann

31. Ibid.
32. Ibid., 311.

assumes this about God, but he is not as clear as he could be in describing how that suffering comes to an end—and when. He writes, "Therefore anyone who enters into love, and through love experiences inextricable suffering and the fatality of death, enters into the history of the human God, for his forsakenness is lifted away from him in the forsakenness of Christ, and in this way he can continue to love."[33] One is left to wonder if and how that love changes the conditions of the world, as Moltmann seems to suggest that it does. Moltmann appears to rest on his own eschatological hope that Christ has paved the way for something new that will eventually be realized in full, but how and when that will happen is left as an open question.

Another important critique of Moltmann's model of the suffering God comes from Dorothee Söelle, who suggests that even though God suffers in and with Jesus, God is still presumed to be in control of the events. That means that God wills and allows Jesus' suffering to take place. According to Söelle, this makes God sadistic and means that Christians worship an executioner.[34] Moltmann responded with horror to this critique, noting that of course God does not endorse the victimization of any sons or daughters. Furthermore, Moltmann points out that Christ's sacrifice ended sacrificial religions—and especially child sacrifice—once and for all,[35] but this response seems to miss Söelle's point. Even if Christ's sacrifice prevented future child sacrifices, that does not change the fact that God ordered, willed, or allowed Christ's death. Because God is still omnipotent in Moltmann's model, there is no getting around the fact that Christ's death remains God's responsibility.

But even if we put aside the accusation that God is a sadist, in Moltmann's model, God does not forcefully renounce suffering. Though it may be comforting to know that God does not will our suffering and that God suffers along with us, Moltmann's model does not adequately explain why God continues to allow this suffering. Moltmann does acknowledge that those who love God will be at odds with the ways of the world, but his model does not explain how God's suffering with us changes the situation or brings suffering to an end.

33. Ibid., *Crucified God*, 254.

34. See Söelle, *Suffering*, 26–27.

35. Moltmann, "Crucified God: Yesterday and Today," 136–37.

Jon Sobrino

Like the previous authors, Sobrino's understanding of God and the work of Christ is molded by his context. He is a Jesuit priest who lives and works in El Salvador, surrounded by extreme poverty and suffering. This context produces a theology that differs greatly from traditional theology that is written in the developed world. Sobrino finds that much so-called First World theology tries to erase the scandal of the cross and explain it away as part of God's plan, but his model refuses to do that. The cross occupies a central position in Sobrino's model because he argues that Jesus' death on the cross is God's way of identifying with those who continue to suffer crucifixions of all kinds in today's world. According to Sobrino, Jesus' death serves as an indictment of certain elements of society, namely the systems of injustice—and those who benefit from such systems—that caused his execution. In both his life and death, "Jesus is *for* some, the oppressed, and *against* others, the oppressors."[36] The point for Sobrino is that Jesus' actions throughout his life and in his suffering and death reveal that God cares especially for those on the underside of society. In fact, not only does God care for them, God identifies with them and even becomes one of them, which is why Jesus lived his life as a peasant who was unable to overcome the systems of power that held him. For Sobrino, Jesus' death on the cross is scandalous, but not because it was *Jesus* who died, but rather because the systems that produced Jesus' cross continue to torture others. He writes, "There is indeed an immense tragedy in this, though not primarily because it happened to Jesus—who was later recognized as the Son of God—but because it occurs to many human beings, also sons and daughters of God."[37] Therefore, Sobrino argues that Jesus' suffering and God's identification with one who suffers is not the end in itself, as it seems to be in Moltmann's model. Instead, Jesus' suffering and God's identification with those who suffer protest and condemn the suffering that others continue to endure.

Sobrino's model highlights the historical Jesus of Nazareth rather than the metaphysical Christ. Therefore, Sobrino pays special attention to the ministry and actions of Jesus and notices that he constantly seeks to subvert the power paradigm and liberate people from their oppression. In fact, Sobrino argues that the whole point of Jesus' mission was to proclaim the kingdom of God—and the kingdom of God is not good

36. Sobrino, *Jesus the Liberator*, 13.

37. Ibid., 210.

news for everyone, because it means overthrowing the systems that keep some people at the bottom and some people at the top of the heap. In other words, this is a preferential kingdom, and that is what was scandalous—and dangerous—about Jesus' message. Sobrino reasons, "For the kingdom of God to come for the just had its own inner logic; that it should come without taking account of individual moral states was a scandal. The proclamation of good news to the poor simply because they were poor shook the very foundations of religion, and was the best way of showing God's gratuitousness in a world that idolized riches."[38] Surely Jesus' message was good news to the poor, but it threatened the position of those in power, and that is precisely why those with power killed him.

According to Sobrino, God does not will Jesus' death, and that death does not cause salvation. Instead, "what God's suffering on the cross says in the end is that the God who fights against human suffering wanted to show solidarity with human beings who suffer."[39] In fact, he argues that Jesus himself did not view his own death as serving some salvific purpose.[40] But he did view his death as being in line with the message of his life. Sobrino reads the Last Supper tradition to mean that Jesus interpreted his death as an act of service that continued the service he offered to others in his life. He writes, "Jesus went to his death with confidence and saw it as a final act of service, more in the manner of an effective example that would motivate others than as a mechanism of salvation for others."[41] In other words, Jesus' death effects salvation only inasmuch as it motivates others to follow his example and identify with the poor and oppressed.

In Sobrino's model, the kingdom or salvation that Jesus offers is not about forgiveness of individual sins. In fact, he argues that traditional theology has collapsed everything that is wrong with humans and our society into this category called sin. But Jesus offers plural salvations: "salvation from any sort of oppression, inner and outer, spiritual and physical, personal and social."[42] Again and again Sobrino emphasizes that what God is doing through Jesus' life and death is identifying with the poor and oppressed and rejecting the systems that keep them in those situa-

38. Ibid., 83.
39. Ibid., 245.
40. Ibid., 201.
41. Ibid., 204.
42. Ibid., 222.

tions. He argues that structural injustice in the form of institutionalized violence is not only the worst sin, but also the worst form of violence, and while Sobrino does not necessarily advocate revolutionary violence to overthrow those systems of injustice, he also does not condemn it. He further warns that those who benefit from those systems should be very careful about being scandalized by such revolutionary violence.[43]

There are many positive aspects of Sobrino's model, especially for those in the Anabaptist tradition. It rests squarely on Jesus' life, ministry, and example and finds in Jesus' ministry a condemnation of the systems that oppress. Jesus' (and God's) attitude toward the injustices of the world means that following Jesus means provoking conflict with those who do not operate with this attitude. Though Sobrino does not advocate a separation from the world the way early Anabaptist theologians did, he does note that those who best manifest God are the least of these, which is consistent with Anabaptist theology.

Not only is Sobrino's model concerned with the history of Jesus, but it also expresses care for the lived history of those in this world. He argues that if Christians want to know who God is and to participate in God's love, they must go to the foot of what he calls "historical crosses,"[44] meaning the places where people continue to suffer injustices. He argues that God's love is found in this world, and God cares about the sufferings endured in this world. Clearly salvation cannot be an otherworldly reward that believers earn by enduring their suffering. Sobrino does not necessarily discount the possibility of heaven, but it is not the focus of his model or of how he interprets Jesus' understanding of the kingdom of God. Instead, salvation primarily concerns the current lived experiences of the poor and oppressed.

Many theologians, including some in the Anabaptist tradition, have critiqued Sobrino's model for not explicitly condemning violence. They argue that Jesus' actions were nonviolent, and therefore Christians' actions should also be nonviolent. However, Sobrino's argument that it is easy to condemn revolutionary violence when one is not being ground to dust under the heel of poverty is fair. Perhaps truly being in solidarity with the poor and oppressed includes openness to using a variety of means to overthrow systems of injustice.[45]

43. Ibid., 215.

44. Ibid., 251.

45. For a complete discussion of why a commitment to complete nonviolence (and therefore non-engagement with the world) may not be the best position for

In a different vein, Sobrino's model seems to contain an inconsistency in that Jesus overcomes sin by bearing it. He argues that sin—real historical sins—caused the death of Jesus, and the fact that Jesus died for our sins really means that he was crushed on a particular historical occasion. But Sobrino goes on to say that what should be done to eradicate sin is to bear it: "And rather than taking on the guilt of sin, bearing the sin of others means bearing the sin's historical effects: being ground down, crushed, put to death."[46] In this way, those in the so-called Third World become "bearers of 'historical soteriology.'"[47] There are two problems with this idea. First, it undermines Sobrino's own openness to overthrowing oppression by means of revolution. Second, it suggests that the suffering of the poor offers salvation to their oppressors, which valorizes the suffering of the poor just as the argument that Jesus' suffering eradicates human sin by bearing it valorizes his suffering. This positive view of suffering seems to contradict Sobrino's argument that God wishes to eradicate not individual sin, but the suffering caused by systemic sin. It seems difficult to simultaneously maintain that Jesus' suffering is the result of unjust systems of oppression *and* that his bearing that suffering dismantles—or at least condemns—those systems.

Wendy Farley

Both Rauschenbusch and Sobrino highlighted the social nature of sin, and Wendy Farley builds on that idea, but she focuses on the individual trapped in social sin and the tools that an individual can utilize for salvation. Whereas Rauschenbusch and Sobrino look to action in the world as a source for redemption, Farley finds wisdom in the monastic tradition that separated itself from society. To be sure, Farley recognizes that sin is larger than mere individuals. She writes, "Emptying Christianity into a narrow pattern of sin and redemption denies us the enormous wisdom this tradition has for interpreting the ways that we as individuals and communities are bound to unloving, destructive patterns of life and relationship."[48] In other words, we are negatively affected by life

---

contemporary Anabaptists to take, see Eisenbise, *For Thy Neighbors' Good*, 116–40.

46. Ibid., 260.

47. Ibid., 261.

48. Farley, *Wounding and Healing*, xix.

patterns—both those of our own making and those much larger than ourselves.

Farley notes that much of the Christian tradition has located the problem of sin in desire—the desire for material gains, for sexual pleasure, for power. But she notes that desire need not be a sinful urge, for at the root of what it means to be human is the desire for relationship with others. She sees desire as a positive human drive rather than the basis for all human sin and suffering. In fact, Farley argues that much of life's suffering is due to the fact that this desire is not fulfilled, not because the desire exists in the first place. She writes, "We feel the solitariness of life so poignantly because desire insists that communion is available to us."[49] Desire is what pushes us toward relationship, which is one of the key aspects of Farley's understanding of salvation. In this way, she reclaims desire as a natural and healthy aspect of what it means to be human and builds her model around the idea that salvation includes the fulfillment of this human desire for relationship.

While Farley reclaims desire as a positive human drive, she has no use for the notion of guilt. She rejects the traditional idea that humanity suffers in this world because we are somehow guilty before God. She acknowledges that the atonement models that blame human suffering on our guilt rather than on God preserve some positive qualities of God. If our suffering is due to our own faults, then God is just and righteous in demanding punishment or satisfaction. But Farley argues that this model hides the true loving nature of God. It also improperly ignores the unjustifiability of much suffering. She writes, "Theologies of cosmic guiltiness are . . . fantasies that obscure the horrific reality that suffering cannot be justified. At the same time, while this guiltiness may preserve God's honor, it disguises from us the infinitely sweet and unstained depths of divine love."[50] Indeed, some of these models turn God into a monster, as many theologians have noted. Moreover, the damage done by models that blame suffering on the victims is enormous and heartbreaking.

According to Farley, all suffering cannot be attributed to our guilt or our desires, but she does not throw away all traditional theology. She recognizes that this theology does offer a good way to talk about the systems and actions that lead to suffering, and she retains the traditional language of sin: "Interpreting injustice as sin serves as a much-needed reminder

49. Ibid., 5.
50. Ibid., 20.

that injustice and the structures that carry it blaspheme the divine image ... Using the language of sin assists us in seeing the seriousness of injustice and to understand it as a religious and spiritual problem rather than a matter of political opinion."[51] But she also argues that the word "sin" carries some negative baggage of its own. Such language tends to convict us in a way that is harmful and that makes compassion for ourselves difficult. Instead, she advocates a model that interprets our "addiction to the causes of evil and suffering as bondage arising out of the deep woundedness of existence."[52] In this way, Farley's model draws attention to the way sin injures us, not just the way sin indicts us and makes us blameworthy.

Though Farley adamantly denounces the valorization of suffering, she does find that something good has come out of Christ's suffering on the cross. She writes, "But because Christ has put Herself on the tip of the sword of affliction, affliction itself can carry Christ into our deepest heart."[53] Christ's action, or our knowledge of his action, certainly does not end our suffering or cause our pain to disappear, but it does show that God (in Christ) is present in our own hell, pouring out love for us, which makes it possible for us to escape, or at least endure, our own hells. The knowledge that God always loves us, no matter what we do, frees us from the obstacles, or what Farley calls "the passions,"[54] so that divine love can flow through us. Horrible things continue to happen in the world, but God's love is still present: "Christ's wounds do not make these things go away. They show us where the Divine Eros is in all of these things ... Christ shows us Erotic power as the power that keeps the story moving toward freedom at every point."[55] And the best way for each person to become aware of that fact that divine love is present everywhere, even in our suffering, is through the practice of contemplation. Contemplation helps us to move more deeply into that divine love. A deeper communion with God leads to a deeper compassion and love for other beings, which in turn dismantles our egocentrism and allows for greater communion with one another.[56] At this point, Farley's model has come full circle. The

51. Ibid., 23. In this way, Farley's model has important points of contact with Rauschenbusch's theory: social injustice is a spiritual or religious problem, and any kind of religious redemption must therefore address this injustice.

52. Ibid., 25.

53. Ibid., 144.

54. Ibid., 35–53.

55. Ibid., 145.

56. Ibid., 115–46, especially 116.

desire for relationship (with others and with God) has been fulfilled, and that is the goal of salvation.

There is much to admire in Farley's model. It highlights the fact that humanity is created out of divine goodness and that we retain that goodness. In other words, she recognizes a high or optimistic theological anthropology, just as Anabaptists have almost always done. She refuses to explain away suffering as an indictment of pride or guilt in some extra-historical narrative. Instead, she takes suffering and pain seriously, and still affirms that God is present in those experiences. Her understanding of sin as egocentrism, or a sort of psychic block that prevents us from becoming aware of our integral connections to one another and to God, certainly makes sense within a postmodern view of the human person.

But from an Anabaptist perspective, Farley's model has two flaws. First, it incorporates important elements of Jesus' life, but those elements do not form the backbone of this model. Indeed, Farley is more likely to speak of the actions of Christ in a generic and metaphysical sense (of Christ calling back Her lovers through an intoxication of desire, for example[57]) than about the concrete historical actions of Jesus. The one notable exception is her understanding of Jesus' temptations. Farley argues that Jesus' temptations in the wilderness were really invitations to grasp worldly power rather than the power of divine love, and this is one of the most persuasive aspects of her entire model.

The other flaw of this model is that although it acknowledges the social character of sin and the human problem of egocentrism and isolation, the solution Farley offers seems to occur in isolation, in contemplation within the monastic tradition. Farley believes that the natural consequence of contemplation will be healed relationships with God and others, so her solution does have a social component, but it seems like the solution itself should be more communal. This belief is especially important for those in the Anabaptist tradition because Anabaptist theology has always affirmed that the best way to experience God is in the community rather than in isolation.

Cynthia Crysdale

Cynthia Crysdale, a Roman Catholic theologian and ethicist, takes seriously the feminist critiques of suffering and especially of the valorization

---

57. Ibid., 29.

of suffering in traditional atonement models. But she refuses to let go of the notion that suffering can sometimes be redemptive. Therefore, her model seeks to hold both assertions together: suffering in the form of victimization can be quite harmful, but suffering in solidarity with another can be transformative and redemptive.

In order to maintain this balance, Crysdale first re-imagines the traditional notion of sin. She argues that sometimes, sin has been defined as betrayal of our true selves,[58] but sin must also include the acceptance of denigration. In other words, we must recognize ourselves as both perpetrators (those who betray their true selves by perpetrating violence or domination) and victims (those who accept denigration by passively suffering at the hands of others) and realize that neither state is acceptable. Crysdale calls this recognition "conversion" or "transformation," and it forms the core of her atonement model.[59]

She argues that traditional theology only addresses perpetrators and counsels them to deny their egos and pride. But this same advice can be harmful to victims. If a person does not have ego or pride in the first place, the advice to divest oneself of power makes no sense. In fact, it can end up making victims' situations even worse. This kind of theology counsels victims to stay silent and to bravely endure their victimization as a path to salvation.[60] Crysdale points out that sin must be defined differently for those without power. For victims, sin is passive compliance with the systems that keep them in such situations. As such, salvation for these people looks different as well: "For the crucified of the world salvation involves finding a voice to declare their humanity in the face of powerful messages to the contrary."[61] This demands a conversion that involves realizing and proclaiming the self as a child of God and then taking responsibility for oneself. As Crysdale explains, "Salvation/healing involves taking responsibility for the consequences of one's conversion

---

58. This definition comes from the theology of Sebastian Moore, which Crysdale both utilizes and critiques (Crysdale, *Embracing Travail*, 8–11). See Moore, *Crucified Is No Stranger*.

59. Crysdale, *Embracing Travail*, 16–17.

60. Crysdale credits womanist thought (especially that of Delores Williams) for this insight, but her critique is also quite similar to that made by Judith Plaskow in her analysis of Reinhold Niebuhr's understanding of sin. See Plaskow, *Sex, Sin, and Grace*, 54–73.

61. Crysdale, *Embracing Travail*, 16.

and following through on whatever public changes may be necessary in one's own life."[62] She argues that this is precisely what Jesus did.

Jesus did not let his ego interfere with his deepest self that was in divine relation. He lived out a new set of values that came from that relationship with God. He recognized the dignity of all and used power in a healing, transformative way. Out of these new values, he chose a radically different way of resisting evil forces. He chose to stop the cycle of revenge by suffering evil rather than by doing evil, and when he did so, he revealed that evil does not destroy divine communion or human integrity. He was not destroyed, but resurrected.

The meaning of that resurrection is two-fold for Crysdale: "There is no evil that we on earth might suffer which is beyond the scope of God's healing and . . . there is no evil on earth we might commit that is beyond the reach of God's forgiveness."[63] She recognizes that the message of the cross and the resurrection has meaning for both victims and perpetrators, and if we are to understand the full message, we must recognize ourselves as both victims and perpetrators. She writes, "Jesus' suffering, death, and resurrection are models of resistance for people of all races and classes who are oppressed. But unless one discovers oneself in Jesus, discovers oneself as both victim and crucifier, this resistance runs the risk of either succumbing to suffering and yielding to the Powers, or turning into a vengeful violence that never establishes justice."[64] When we recognize ourselves on both sides of the cross, we may discover new insights, and we may even be provoked to work to change oppressive structures.

But in our efforts to change these structures, we must remember that we do not have the power to completely overhaul the domination system. We can only do so much in the face of such a powerful system. Even Jesus faced such limitations. According to Crysdale, "He took what action he could, realizing that its objective was not a final solution but a setting up of the conditions of possibility for transformation."[65] Here, Crysdale argues against the notion that we can build the kingdom of God by ourselves. She adamantly maintains that the true kingdom requires God's grace, but she distinguishes between "operative grace" and

---

62. Ibid., 17. However, Crysdale also notes that taking responsibility for oneself is certainly not the same as accepting the blame of the oppressor.

63. Ibid., 30.

64. Ibid., 55.

65. Ibid., 57.

"cooperative grace."[66] Operative grace is God's action in the world, but it need not be thought of as God's interventionist action. Rather, sudden insights or "aha!" moments are examples of operative grace. She argues that these insights do not come from within ourselves; they must come from God. But insights alone do not change the world. They require our cooperative grace, or a response to these insights. We are the ones who must convert the insights into actions that set up the conditions for the possibility of transformation. In this way, Crysdale's model takes on an important role for the believer.

Crysdale's model succeeds on many points. Her analysis of different kinds of sin (wielding power over others as well as accepting the denigration of self) offers a compelling alternative to the traditional notion of sin, and her description of salvation for victims proposes a necessary corrective to many traditional views of salvation as only heaven. Her advice that all people must recognize themselves as both victims and crucifiers is a great insight, because although almost everyone is fully aware of the ways we are oppressed by others, most of us have a large blind spot when it comes to recognizing our complicity in systems that oppress others. However, one wonders whether Crysdale jumps to this acknowledgement that we are all victims and perpetrators too quickly—that is, in a way that allows perpetrators to say to victims, "Yes, well, you're perpetrators too!" Though Crysdale argues that we must all take responsibility for our different kinds of sin, it seems that she should take into account Jon Sobrino's claim that Jesus was not for all people equally. While it may be true that all of us are perpetrators and victims, some of us victimize more often than we are victims.

Crysdale describes her own model as trying to balance a critique of suffering with the acknowledgement that suffering can sometimes be redemptive, and she does that most elegantly in her description of what it means to be in solidarity with others. Here, she argues that solidarity of course entails honest communication, finding common ground, listening to others, etc., "But unless one is also facing oneself, open to discovering the nature of one's wounds and to taking responsibility for one's oppressive actions, such conversations can backfire."[67] In other words, sharing the ways we are all victims and sinners opens up the conversation in new ways and does not polarize different groups by labeling one as oppressors

66. Ibid., 33–37.
67. Ibid., 65.

and the other as the oppressed. As a result of honest communication, we cannot help but suffer with others as we experience their heartbreaks. But "this 'suffering with' cannot be either a projection or an introjection of others' pain into our own lives: this simply mimics the tactics of the domination/suffering cycle. The compassion required for solidarity must begin with owning one's own pain and recognizing one's complicity in it. *Out* of such pain and recognition of sin one can then genuinely enter into the passion of another."[68] In this way, Crysdale argues that suffering just for the sake of suffering does not help anything. But *suffering with* others may be a powerful and transformative action.

Walter Wink

Though Walter Wink has written numerous books on many aspects of Christian theology, he is most famous for his *The Powers* trilogy, a series of books that seeks to explain evil in a way that makes sense to modern believers. He refuses to completely demythologize the powers and principalities that Paul describes (Eph 6:12) as "just" human institutions and systems. Rather, Wink understands that these institutions and systems have an inner spiritual essence. He explains that "the 'demons' are the psychic or spiritual power emanated by organizations or individuals or subaspects of individuals whose energies are bent on overpowering others."[69] Wink recognizes that these powers are greater than the actions, energies, or systems of individual humans; once these actions, energies, or systems gain enough force, they start to take on a life of their own, and these powers work together to form what Wink calls the "domination system." As Wink explains, "The Domination System is the outcome of the systemic repudiation by institutions of their divine vocations in order to pursue self-aggrandizement and greed."[70] The work of Jesus was to resist this system at every turn, but not by using power and force like the domination system does. Instead, he engaged those who suffered under this system and offered a new way of living. He preached a message of God's domination-free order. Wink writes, "What makes Jesus' message so powerful, however, is that he did not articulate it as an ideal, unattainable in this world and to be passively awaited in the distant future. He

---

68. Ibid., emphasis in original.

69. Wink, *Unmasking the Powers*, 104.

70. Ibid., 107.

lived it. He acted on it. He brought it to reality by actually freeing people from bondage."[71] This freedom from bondage was not some metaphorical freedom from Satan's control; instead, it was freedom to explore the new strategies Jesus suggested for retaining their dignity under the domination system.

Wink is perhaps most famous for his description of what he calls Jesus' third way, or nonviolent direct action, a concept many Christians are likely familiar with even if they do not know who first proposed it.[72] Wink argues that Jesus' advice to his followers to turn the other cheek, give their cloak too, and go the second mile (Matt 5:38–42 and Luke 6:29–30) was not instruction to let oppressors perpetrate evil unopposed. Jesus did not teach his followers to be doormats. Wink points out that Jesus' audience was made up of those on the underside of power relationships; they were the ones who repeatedly suffered humiliation at the hands of their so-called superiors, so Jesus' directive gave these people nonviolent ways to reclaim their dignity. In each of these situations, "he is helping an oppressed people find a way to protest and neutralize an onerous practice despised throughout the empire. He is not giving a nonpolitical message of spiritual world transcendence. He is formulating a worldly spirituality in which the people at the bottom of society or under the thumb of imperial power learn to recover their humanity."[73] We will examine each of these sayings in turn to determine how it enables the subjugated to recover their dignity.

First, Jesus says, "If anyone strikes you on the right cheek, turn the other also" (Matt 5:39). Wink points out that it is no coincidence that Jesus specifically mentions the right cheek here. If a superior strikes an inferior on the right cheek, he does so with a backhanded slap, a gesture meant to reinforce humiliation and submission. But if the inferior person presents his left cheek to also be hit, the striker has a difficult decision to make. He cannot strike his inferior with the back of his left hand because no one used the left hand in public. He cannot backhand the left cheek with his right hand because it is incredibly physically awkward. (As Wink points out, one need only try this to see the problem.) His only option is to strike the left cheek with his right fist. But in the culture of the day, one only hit an equal with a closed-fist punch. Therefore, if Jesus' audience

71. Wink, *Engaging the Powers*, 135.

72. For a complete discussion of Jesus' third way, see ibid., 175–93.

73. Ibid., 182.

were to follow his unusual advice, they would essentially say to their in-
feriors, "Try again. Your first blow failed to achieve its intended effect. I
deny you the power to humiliate me. I am a human being just like you.
Your status does not alter that fact. You cannot demean me."[74] In this way,
the victim acts nonviolently, simply by moving his or her head, but the
effect is powerful: the victim regains personal agency in the situation by
asserting his or her self-respect rather than cowering before the blow.

Jesus' second example is set in a courtroom where someone is being
sued for his cloak, and Jesus teaches that he should give over his under-
shirt as well (Matt 5:40). Wink argues that this vignette is Jesus' critique
of an economic system that trapped peasants in cycles of crushing poverty. We can imagine the courtroom situation. The debtor has no legal
recourse. All of the cards are stacked against him, and there is no way he
can repay his debt. In order to show the absurdity of the situation and
of the system that trapped him in it, the man strips naked to show that
he has been stripped of everything he has. Once again, the tables have
been turned. The debtor essentially says, "You want my robe? Here, take
everything! Now you've got all I have except my body. Is that what you'll
take next?"[75] He has transcended his own shame to shame the creditor
instead—both because the creditor is not following Jewish law, which
requires the return of the collateral of the very poorest of the poor before
sundown, and because within Judaism, shame falls less on the naked person than on the person viewing a naked body. The debtor's unmasking of
the system's cruelty allows the creditor to see, perhaps for the first time,
how unjust the system from which he benefits truly is.

Finally, the third situation involves carrying a soldier's pack for two
miles rather than the required one (Matt 5:41). Wink explains that Roman soldiers had to carry their own packs of supplies, which could weigh
as much as eighty-five pounds. To help them carry this burden, they were
legally allowed to conscript citizens to haul it for them, but in order to
limit abuses of non-military citizens, no one could be conscripted to carry a pack for more than a mile. The punishment for a soldier who forced
someone to carry his pack for more than a mile ranged from a mild ver-
bal rebuke to death. According to Wink, the point is that the soldiers
never knew the punishment they might get for such an action. Therefore,
when the conscripted person cheerfully requests to carry the pack for a

74. Ibid., 176.
75. Ibid., 179.

second mile, he puts the soldier in an unexpected and uncomfortable position. Wink writes, "He has never dealt with such a problem before. Now he has been forced into making a decision for which nothing in his previous experience has prepared him. If he has enjoyed feeling superior to the vanquished, he will not enjoy it today. Imagine the situation of a Roman infantryman pleading with a Jew to give back his pack!"[76] Once again, Jesus' advice on how to manage this situation gives agency and dignity to the oppressed person.

According to Wink, the point of these three sayings is that Jesus instructs his followers to stand up for themselves—not in a violent revolutionary way that will only get them killed, but in small ways that allow them to reclaim their own self-worth. Too often, these sayings have been preached in a way that instructs Christians to suffer injustices in order to build up treasure in heaven, but Wink argues that this interpretation could not be further from Jesus' point. Rather than talking about heaven, Jesus is giving those on the underside strategies to unmask and disrupt the powers that be. In fact, for Wink, this is Jesus' primary purpose.

Wink understands Jesus' death through the lens of the *Christus Victor* theory. He argues that Jesus' death challenged the entire domination system because it exposes the weakness of the powers: "The Powers threw at him every weapon in their arsenal. But they could not deflect him from the trail that he and God were blazing. Because he lived thus, we too can find our path."[77] In other words, Jesus' truth and God's will for a domination-free society could not be killed, even as Jesus himself was killed. Instead, Jesus' willing acceptance of his death and his refusal to react violently to save himself inspired others to live into his vision of a domination-free society. Wink's description of this phenomenon is captivating: "Killing Jesus was like trying to destroy a dandelion seed-head by blowing on it."[78] In this way, the message of Jesus (and the will of God) lives on and gains victory over the powers that be.

Wink's work in explicating the powers and how they work in our world has won him numerous book awards, and contemporary theology has surely benefited from these ideas. His description of Jesus' third way lifts up several positive themes: Jesus'/God's condemnation of oppression and care for the oppressed, an emphasis on Jesus' life and ministry as

76. Ibid., 182.

77. Ibid., 141.

78. Ibid., 143.

well as a focus on this world, and an awareness of social or corporate sin (i.e., the powers). His view that salvation has something to do with life here and now is attractive and seems to be in keeping with elements of Anabaptist thought. Yet Wink's model has one major problem: it is basically a reinterpretation of the *Christus Victor* theory. Though it is an appealing reinterpretation in many ways, it falls prey to the same critiques as the classical theory. The same questions remain as to how the powers will ultimately be defeated (since they are still very clearly at work in our world) and why God does not bring about that victory immediately. For these reasons, it seems that we may need to move past any reliance on the *Christus Victor* theory and instead weave some of Wink's insights into a different model.

Marcus Borg

Marcus Borg has become one of the leading theologians for progressive Christianity, and his model addresses some of the problems posed by traditional theories of atonement we noted in the previous chapter. First, he acknowledges that there is something wrong with humanity, though he wonders whether sin is the best way to describe the problem. He suggests that Christianity seems obsessed with sin and forgiveness, but the human problem is not always healed by forgiveness. He writes, "If the issue is blindness, what we need is not forgiveness, but sight. If the issue is bondage, what we need is not forgiveness, but liberation, and so forth."[79] Second, sin is usually conceived as an individual problem, and that concept obscures much of what is wrong with human society. As Borg points out, "it wasn't individual sins that caused Jesus' death. He wasn't killed because of the impure thoughts of adolescents or our everyday deceptions or our selfishness."[80] In this way, Borg echoes the idea of many contemporary theologians that sin is larger than individual actions; it necessarily includes a social or corporate dimension.

Borg also contends that the typical understanding of salvation falls short of the mark because it is almost always associated with going to heaven. This emphasis on heaven turns Christianity into a religion of

79. Borg, *Heart of Christianity*, 168. Borg illustrates this point well using the story of Israel's enslavement in Egypt: "I have sometimes remarked that if Moses had gone into Egypt and said to the Hebrew slaves, 'My children, your sins are forgiven,' they would have said, 'Well, that's nice, but you see, our problem is bondage'" (ibid., 169).

80. Ibid., 171.

requirements, namely what one has to do to get into heaven. It also creates division within the Christian community between the in-group and an out-group (those who have met the requirements and are going to heaven versus those who have not and are not). Finally, this obsession with heaven focuses our attention on the next world rather than on the transformation of this world.[81] Almost a century later, Borg makes much the same argument that Rauschenbusch did: Christianity cannot simply promise heavenly reward; it must demand the transformation of life here and now. He further points out that salvation in the Bible is almost always understood as a this-worldly phenomenon, and it necessarily has social or communal implications. For Borg, "Salvation is about life together. Salvation is about peace and justice within the community and beyond community . . . The Bible is not about the saving of individuals for heaven, but about a new social and personal reality in the midst of this life."[82] Therefore, Borg pushes Christians towards a new understanding of salvation, and he adamantly rejects the idea that salvation was purchased or otherwise procured by Jesus' blood.

Regarding what traditional theology has taught about Jesus' crucifixion and death, Borg contends that much of it is "bad theology and bad history."[83] He argues that what the Bible has to say on this topic is metaphorical speech rather than factual reporting and that traditional theology has flattened the meaning of Jesus' life and death by insisting that the metaphors be understood historically. Where he takes the most intense exception to traditional theology is with the idea that Jesus' death had to happen. Though some biblical writers describe Jesus' death as necessary, Borg maintains that these are "retrospective and retrojective interpretations."[84] These writers were trying to make sense of Jesus' death, and so they inserted their post-resurrection faith into the narrative as if this were the disciples' and Jesus' own interpretation of the events as they were happening. Borg then argues, "This easily generates the inference that Jesus' death had to happen. But this is not a necessary inference."[85] Borg flatly rejects the idea that God willed the torture and execution of a righteous man, arguing that Jesus' life did not have to end in this hor-

81. Ibid., 172.
82. Ibid., 178, 179.
83. Borg, "Executed by Rome," 158.
84. Ibid., 159.
85. Ibid., 160.

rible fashion, for it was not foreordained by God. But he does acknowledge that Jesus' death was a human inevitability because of the way our systems of domination work. Here Borg follows Wink and many other theologians who have acknowledged that how Jesus was killed is an important indication of the purpose or goal of his ministry, or as Borg calls it, his "passion."[86]

In Christian theology, any reference to Jesus' passion usually refers to his suffering and death, but Borg argues that Jesus was passionate for the kingdom of God:

> His passion, his message, was about the kingdom of God. He spoke to peasants as a voice of religious protest against the central economic and political institutions of his day. He attracted a following, took his movement to Jerusalem at the season of Passover, and there challenged the authorities with public acts and public debates. All of this was his passion, what he was passionate about—God and the kingdom of God, God and God's passion for justice.[87]

This passion for justice led Jesus to oppose the many systems of oppression in his day, and this opposition to power is what got him killed. After all, "this is what domination systems do to people who challenge them, publicly and vigorously."[88] Borg argues that the purpose of Jesus' life was not to die, but that the purpose of his life—that is, working to expose and condemn injustice—led to his death. He states this paradox well: "Did Good Friday have to happen? As divine necessity? No. As human inevitability? Virtually."[89]

Following this train of thought, Borg argues that Jesus acted as a sacrifice, but not as a substitute for all of humanity. Biblical writers do not automatically make this assumption, nor do we in everyday language. Borg points out that we often talk about the sacrifices of people who give up their lives—of soldiers who die for their countries or figures like Martin Luther King Jr. and Mahatma Gandhi, who sacrificed their lives for their causes—but never do we assume that these people acted as our substitutes.[90] Similarly, we need not understand Jesus' death as foreordained

86. Ibid., 161.
87. Ibid.
88. Ibid., 160.
89. Ibid., 161.
90. Ibid., 157.

by God to stand in our place and receive our punishment. Borg argues that the best way to understand Jesus' death is simply that he was killed by the domination systems he opposed throughout his lifetime. In this way, Borg follows Wink's theology closely.

Many aspects of Borg's atonement theology are appealing, such as his argument for the reality of social sin, for salvation to include more than simply a ticket to heaven, and that Jesus' death was not foreordained by God for the forgiveness of sins. But perhaps the greatest impact of Borg's writing is that it gives Christians permission to let much of traditional theology go in search of new ideas that make more sense in the contemporary world. Perhaps a problem with Borg's model is that some details are missing, such as a clear explanation of what—if anything—Jesus' death accomplishes, or exactly what salvation looks like, or what role believers have to play in that salvation. But this lack of detail in Borg's incomplete model could also be viewed as a strength because it recognizes that the Bible and the Christian tradition have yielded multiple ideas about Jesus and his death and salvation. By refusing to iron out all the wrinkles, Borg avoids the trap of working out a logical and complete system of atonement that sacrifices the notion of a loving and righteous God. Borg's model may be a little fuzzy, but at least it revolves around a God worthy of worship.

Although Borg and the other theologians examined in this chapter vary in their backgrounds and in their ideas, I have included them in this discussion because each of their models offers something that may be appealing for a Brethren view of atonement. We will pick up these themes again in chapter 5, but first it will be helpful to analyze contemporary Anabaptist theories of atonement. The models in the following chapter will take up some of the themes highlighted in this chapter, as well as those distinctive elements of traditional Anabaptist theology highlighted in chapter 1.

CHAPTER 4

Contemporary Anabaptist Models of Atonement

In chapter 1, we saw that Anabaptist soteriology differs somewhat from the mainline Protestant tradition. As we have seen, early Anabaptists combined an emphasis on salvation by grace through faith with the expectation that the inner rebirth (God's gift through the Holy Spirit) would be reflected in an outer life of discipleship (the human response that necessarily results from God's gift of rebirth). In this way, sixteenth-century Anabaptism navigated between Catholic and Protestant understandings of salvation, incorporating elements of each. Contemporary Anabaptist soteriology, with its emphasis on faith and discipleship, continues to offer a corrective to much modern atonement theory (especially that which comes out of an Anselmian satisfaction tradition) that neglected to include an ethical component. Anabaptist scholar Arnold Snyder suggests the following synthesis of sixteenth-century and contemporary Anabaptist contributions to Christian soteriology:

> In a world in which one hears the insistent call to be spiritually 'born again,' an experience which apparently changes one's heavenly status with no corresponding necessity for a life in conformity with the life of Christ, the challenge of Anabaptist spirituality remains clear. The spiritual rebirth of which the Anabaptists spoke was indivisibly linked to a radical discipleship. In the second place, Anabaptist spirituality was premised on the loving presence and powerful action of the Spirit of God,

regenerating and empowering believers. It is the power of God
that makes disciples, and not simply human intentions.[1]

Contemporary theologians who come out of this tradition therefore construct models of atonement or understandings of salvation that
look a bit different from the models analyzed in the previous chapter.
They rework classical models in order to preserve the special emphases
of their Anabaptist ancestors, namely following the way of Jesus through
discipleship. As such, each emphasizes the subjective nature of atonement. This chapter will examine the theories of many important contemporary Anabaptist theologians, starting with the towering figure of John
Howard Yoder, perhaps the most well-known contemporary Anabaptist
theologian.

John Howard Yoder

Yoder's Christology hinges on the belief that Jesus' actions reveal the will
of God. This foundational belief has two implications. First, Jesus' life
and ministry are vitally important because that is where we see God's
will played out on earth. Second, even though Yoder finds Jesus' human
actions to be crucial, Jesus' divinity (his special relationship to God) is
equally important. He writes, "This will of God is affirmatively, concretely
knowable in the person and ministry of Jesus. [However,] Jesus is not to
be looked at merely as the last and greatest in a long line of rabbis teaching pious people how to behave; he is to be looked at as a mover of history
and as the standard by which Christians must learn how they are to look
at the moving of history."[2] In other words, Christian faith is dependent
on the belief that Jesus is Lord, and the actions that result from that faith
are dependent on Jesus' human example.

Yoder believes that Jesus' work as the Christ has two major elements. First, Christ defeats the powers and frees humanity from bondage to them.[3] Second, Christ reveals God's desire for communion with
humanity, as well as God's refusal to infringe on human freedom. The two
theories seem to be relatively unrelated. Yoder discusses Christ's defeat
of the powers in his *The Politics of Jesus* as part of his effort to show that

1. Snyder, *Following in the Footsteps*, 185.

2. Yoder, *Politics of Jesus*, 233.

3. Like Wink, Yoder employs the language of "the powers," drawing upon the
scholarship of Hendrick Berkhof. See Berkhof, *Christ and the Powers*.

Jesus' actions are relevant to a contemporary world ruled by institutions and invisible power structures. The second part of Christ's work—calling humanity back into communion with God—is more like a typical atonement theory, and it is drawn from Yoder's *Preface to Theology*, in which he discusses other theories of atonement. In this work, Yoder offers an alternative understanding of atonement that he thinks corrects some of the negative elements of other theories. Therefore, these two elements of Yoder's soteriology seem to serve slightly different purposes in his writings, but they are both fundamental to Yoder's view of Christ's work in the world.

Defeat of the Powers

Yoder recognizes that we live in a world of power and structures (or power structures), but he rejects the argument that Jesus' actions cannot be applicable to this kind of world. Instead, he argues that this is exactly the world that Paul describes with his language of the powers and principalities.[4] After discussing the difficulty regarding the ambiguity of the language used to describe these structures, Yoder eventually defines the structures as the divinely ordained reign of order among creatures. These structures, or powers, are necessary for life to exist, and they were created by God as a good part of creation and given as a gift. They provide regularity and a systematic order for society, history, and even nature.[5]

However, despite the powers' original goodness, they rebelled and are now fallen. Whereas they used to function as mediators of the saving creative purpose of God, they now seek to separate humanity from the love of God. Rather than ordering and supporting life so that humans can worship and be in communion with God, the powers now insert themselves in his place to seek worship for themselves. Instead of the powers serving humanity, humans have becomes slaves to them, for the powers have claimed the status of idols and have succeeded in making humans think that they are of absolute value. Yoder writes, "These structures which were supposed to be our servants have become our masters."[6]

Yet despite their fallenness, the powers continue to exercise their ordering function in the world, and God can continue to use them for

4. Ibid., 134–36.
5. Ibid., 136–37, 141.
6. Ibid., 141.

good. The powers cannot simply be destroyed or ignored because they are what allow and enable human existence. Instead, the powers' sovereignty must be broken, and humanity must be released from bondage. Yoder claims that "this is what Jesus did, concretely and historically, by living a genuinely free and human existence."[7] Like every other person, Jesus was subordinate to these powers, for he lived within the history and society they make possible, "But morally he broke their rules by refusing to support them in their self-glorification; and that is why they killed him."[8] Jesus was not a slave of any power, law, custom, community, institution, value, or theory, even when to do so would have saved his own life. Jesus broke the powers' authority by making a public example of them, by triumphing over them, and by disarming them.[9]

First, Jesus made a public example of the powers. He revealed that the powers are not the most basic and ultimate realities in the world when he offered himself as a comparison. When compared to God in Christ, the powers are exposed as his adversaries and as idols: "They are unmasked as false gods by their encounter with Very God; they are made a public spectacle."[10] In this way, Christ triumphed over the powers because this unmasking is actually their defeat. The resurrection provides an additional layer of defeat, for "The resurrection manifests what was already accomplished at the cross: that in Christ God challenged the Powers, has penetrated into their territory, and has displayed that He is stronger than they."[11] Thus, Christ also disarmed the powers. He removed their weapon of illusion, "their ability to convince us that they were the divine regents of the world, ultimate certainty and ultimate direction, ultimate happiness and the ultimate duty for small, dependent humanity."[12]

In other words, Christ unmasks the powers as false gods and allows humans to see the true God. However, although Christ is lord over history, the powers do not yet recognize his lordship.[13] They continue to act as fallen entities; they continue to attract human beings into bondage.

7. Ibid., 144–45.

8. Ibid., 145.

9. Yoder takes most of this explanation of Jesus' defeat of the Powers from Berkhof's *Christ and the Powers*, although he also credits G. B. Caird, G. H. C. MacGregor, and Markus Barth.

10. Berkhof, *Christ and the Powers*, 30, quoted in Yoder, *Politics of Jesus*, 146.

11. Yoder, *Politics of Jesus*, 146.

12. Ibid., 147.

13. Sawatsky, "John Howard Yoder," 252.

Yet Christians, because of what Christ accomplished on the cross (the unmasking of the false claim to authority of the Powers), are able to see the powers for what they truly are. Their role is not to defeat the powers, because they know that Jesus already did that. Instead, Christians' job is to hold the powers—their seduction and enslavement—at a distance. They do this by remaining close to Jesus, following his example in obedience, and voluntarily participating in the church whose role is to witness to Jesus' defeat of the powers.

Yoder's Atonement Theory

Part of Christ's work was to defeat the Powers, but this is not the whole of Yoder's atonement theory. After discussing the negative aspects of other theories of atonement,[14] Yoder lists the following characteristics

14. Although Yoder finds several positive elements to Anselm's satisfaction theory (It answers the question, it takes sin seriously, and it is capable of integrating various biblical imageries, especially sacrifice and redemption.), it nevertheless contains what Yoder views as major flaws. He argues that the theory is not biblical. The New Testament affirms that God is the agent of reconciliation, not the object as in Anselm's theory (Yoder, *Preface to Theology*, 298–90). Also, whereas Anselm makes sin the real problem of atonement, the New Testament sees separation from God and incapacity to do the good as the problem. Yoder writes, "Thus salvation is not primarily the remission of guilt or the cancellation of punishment; it is reconciliation (reestablishment of communion) and obedience, that is, discipleship" (Yoder, *Preface to Theology*, 300). Thus, Yoder argues that in both the Old and New Testaments, forgiveness is a gift of God's grace; it is not something that can be earned by sacrifice.

From the point of view of discipleship, Anselm's theory makes no required link between the cross of Christ and the Christian's obedience or acceptance of the cross. Anselm's theory downplays the necessity of discipleship. Also, it does not make a connection between salvation and the life of Jesus and his obedience. The net effect is that "obedience is not linked to salvation for people, and salvation is not linked to the obedient life of Jesus" (Reesor-Taylor, "Yoder's Mischievous Contribution," 307).

Yoder is also not satisfied with Abelard's Moral Influence theory. First, Yoder argues that the cross of Jesus was a social issue rather than a personal matter that affects only individuals. Yoder argues that this theory likens Jesus to a therapist or counselor who helps people to break through their own self-concerns, defensiveness, and preoccupation with their own self-righteousness. This is not the picture of Jesus that Yoder finds in the New Testament. He writes, "Jesus was judgmental . . . Jesus got in people's way and told them they were doing wrong. He told them to stop and turn around. He did not tell them they were accepted as they were" (Yoder, *Preface to Theology*, 327). In other words, Jesus was divisive, and he demanded action and obedience that would cause disruption in the follower's life. Finally, Yoder also had problems with other themes of atonement such as propitiation, expiation, reparation, and penalty because he felt that although they all try to understand the cross, none of them seem to be

of an adequate atonement theory: The theory must take sin and lost-ness seriously. It must be consonant with the Bible; it should not distort biblical imagery nor be tied to only one symbolic image (like Anselm's dependence on the courtroom analogy). It must somehow be linked to the incarnation, with its double meaning of genuine humanity and genu-ine divine presence. It must somehow recognize Jesus' actions within the political and cultural situation of Palestine, or in other words, must take account of Jesus' particular human life and ministry. It must also place adequate emphasis on the resurrection. Finally, a good theory of atone-ment demands a response from believers. It must call them to obedience and discipleship.[15]

After listing these elements of a good theory, Yoder proposes his own model, which highlights human freedom and God's *agape*. Yoder argues that the problem of evil exists because God created us to pos-sess freedom and personality. In order for us to be truly free, we must be allowed to disobey. We were created for free and obedient communion with God, but we have turned away from God and God's loving gift. Our disobedience has caused a rupture of communion with God, which leads to our inability to do good and love our neighbor. Therefore, the question of atonement asks how God can bring humanity back to communion and obedience (i.e., how God can save us) and at the same time leave human-ity free and respect the hold of human sinfulness. It must answer how God can reveal divine love without forcing it on us, because such force would contradict the nature of divine love.[16] Stated another way, how can God call us back to obedience and communion while still allowing us the option to disobey?

Yoder answers this question by drawing on the nonresistant nature of God's *agape* and Christ's work of obedience. He argues that God's *agape* respects the freedom of the beloved, even to the point that the beloved loses him or herself.[17] Therefore, Christ's work of calling humanity back to God had to be nonresistant. He could not have forced anyone to do anything. Yoder writes, "If Christ had done anything in the face of hu-

---

directly biblical (ibid., 289).

15. Ibid., 289, 306–307.

16. Ibid., 310.

17. Ibid. For this reason, Yoder absolutely rejects the idea of universalism. To assume that all people will somehow, sometime be saved radically undercuts human freedom. It does not take seriously the fact that God's *agape* respects humanity's free-dom to disobey forever, even if it means that person is lost forever.

manity's sinfulness other than to be nonresistant, respecting the freedom to sin against him, his work would have been less than perfect *agape*."[18] Instead, Jesus was nonresistant even when it cost his life. Yoder argues that to be the victim of murder is the utmost act of non-self-defense as well as the utmost in *agape* because it respects the murderer's freedom to commit the worst sin. Therefore, Jesus was obedient to God's *agape* and lovingly respected the freedom of the sinner-murderer to the point that he sacrificed his life: "His sinlessness, his obedience, is what he offered to God, and that sinlessness, utter faithfulness to love, cost his life in a world of sinners."[19] In this way, sacrifice, obedience, and communion with God are identical.

Yoder claims that the cross reveals Jesus' nonresistant *agape*, but it also manifests both the love and wrath of God. He does not equate God's wrath with anger over being dishonored or disobeyed. Rather, Yoder argues that this wrath is the outworking of the process that ensues when we turn against God. In other words, what we experience as God's wrath is the hell that we sink into when we remove ourselves from communion with God. Yoder claims that those who reject the love of God made manifest in the life, death, and resurrection of Christ abandon themselves to utter self-destruction.[20] Hell is not torment as punishment for broken laws; instead, it is leaving people in the isolation from God and humanity that they have chosen: "The only reason for hell is that people persist in a rebellion for which there is no good reason . . . It is just the seriousness of being human that the choices you make are final choices, permanent choices, and God will respect that . . . Part of God's triumph includes the promise not to bulldoze or steamroller people who have chosen to resist."[21]

Although Yoder does not overtly emphasize the resurrection (or perhaps not as much as he should), it is crucial to the rest of his theology, especially his understanding of Christian ethics. Yoder argues that the resurrection was first a simple ontological necessity: death could not hold Jesus down. However, God's resurrection of Jesus also vindicates the rightness, possibility, and ultimate effectiveness of the way of the cross. The resurrection proves that Jesus' nonresistant sacrifice was pleasing to

18. Ibid., 311.
19. Ibid.
20. Ibid., 320.
21. Ibid., 280.

God and that it is indicative of the way God's *agape* functions: "The resurrection proves that, even when humanity does its worst, turns the farthest from God's communion, so far as to kill God, we cannot destroy that love. Humanity has done its worst and the love of God is still stronger; it withstands the assault of sin *without* canceling the sinner's freedom, and it still comes out on top."[22] In spite of the apparent weakness of *agape* in the face of evil, God reigns.[23] The resurrection proves that Jesus is indeed lord over the cosmos, and that although the way of nonresistant *agape* does not appear to be very effective in the world, it is the way of God, the God who is ultimately in control of the universe.

As is typical of Anabaptists, Yoder refuses to separate salvation from ethics or belief from practice. As such, the way of life, or discipleship, is a crucial religious issue. Discipleship is not peripheral or secondary to spirituality or dogma, nor can it be separated from a belief in Christ.[24] For Yoder, to believe in the incarnation is to believe that Jesus' way reveals God's will for the world. He writes, "We are not only asked to believe in Jesus but also to follow him, and it is a mistake to think that belief is intelligible apart from a faithfully lived life."[25]

Although Jesus provides a relatively clear pattern for Christian discipleship, Yoder does not claim that we are expected to resemble Jesus in every way. As Gayle Gerber Koontz explains, "For Yoder that means that what Jesus does about human conflict, community, and social power is normative for Christian ethics in a way that other aspects of his life and teaching are not."[26] That is, we are only asked to imitate Jesus' way of living out the indiscriminating, nonresistant, unconditional character of God's love. Jesus' followers are called to act differently than the world; we are called to witness to the coming of the kingdom.

Jesus' followers are not to imitate the rulers of the world who "lord it over" their people (Matt. 20:25). We are called to do something else, something that is represented in the servant messiah.[27] Therefore, the pattern of faithful obedience we are to follow entails a break with the

22. Ibid., 312, emphasis in original.

23. Koontz, "Confessional Theology," 74.

24. See Nation, *John Howard Yoder*, 104; and Huebner, "Mennonites and Narrative Theology," 26.

25. Yoder, *Preface to Theology*, 17.

26. Koontz, "Confessional Theology," 82.

27. Yoder, *Priestly Kingdom*, 156.

continuities of human civilizations and the loyalties of human societies.[28] True discipleship involves renouncing domination and imitating Jesus' vulnerable love of enemies. It means a "conscious renunciation of the temptation to impose one's will on another's through superior power (Christ's servanthood teaching and example), and affirms the meaningfulness of suffering in conflict (the cross and resurrection)."[29]

Yoder argues that true discipleship will most likely bring suffering, just as Jesus' own actions resulted in suffering. He claims that Jesus' suffering is a result of his renunciation of lordship, his abandonment of earthly security, and the world's antagonistic response to the threat that the Suffering Servant poses to the powerful of the world.[30] Jesus' suffering and death was the price of social nonconformity and the social reality of representing the kingdom in an unwilling world.[31] Yoder is careful to say that it is not the suffering itself that is salvific. He claims that Christian suffering is not the result of misbehavior, but rather the result of conformity with the path of Christ. Suffering comes because of loyalty to Jesus and nonconformity to the world.[32] To be a disciple means sharing in a lifestyle that can culminate in the cross. He writes, "The disciples' cross is not a metaphor for self-mortification or even generally for innocent suffering: 'if you follow me, your fate will be like mine, the fate of a revolutionary. You cannot follow me without facing that fate.'"[33] In other words, to obey God's call to discipleship means risking the same suffering that Jesus endured. Imitating Jesus' love toward his enemies entails the possibility of vulnerability and self-sacrifice.

This willingness to risk suffering and to sacrifice the self in service to God's *agape* is a familiar theme in most Anabaptist theology, and there is surely much to recommend it, given that it does seem to be modeled after Jesus' own example. But the feminist and womanist critiques of suffering and of any atonement model that encourages (or at least condones) suffering still ring in our ears. Although Yoder's model differs from the classic models, it does still require suffering because nonresistant love (which often leads to suffering) is the way of God. Is there a way to maintain

---

28. Ibid., *Royal Priesthood*, 172.
29. Koontz, "Confessional Theology," 82.
30. Yoder, *Politics of Jesus*, 127.
31. Ibid., 96.
32. Ibid., *Royal Priesthood*, 86–87.
33. Ibid., *Politics of Jesus*, 38 n. 28.

this ethic of nonresistant love while also recognizing the dangers of theologically prescribed suffering? We will take up this task in the following chapter. But first, let us move on to examine the atonement theory of another important Mennonite theologian, J. Denny Weaver. Although he never identifies it as such, Yoder's model clearly fits in the *Christus Victor* category of theories. Weaver, by contrast, clearly places his model in that category, though he distinguishes it from the classic theory in that his is *narrative Christus Victor*.

J. Denny Weaver

Whereas John Howard Yoder is probably the most famous Mennonite theologian, Denny Weaver is perhaps the most well-known Anabaptist theologian working specifically in the area of atonement theory. Weaver discards the Anselmian satisfaction model of atonement on several counts, all of which are linked to the distinctive Anabaptist elements discussed earlier. First, he rejects the idea that God and humanity are reconciled by a violent death. Instead, Weaver believes that Jesus' nonresistant way of life reveals the true nonviolent nature of God. As such, "if Jesus truly reveals God the Father, then it would be a contradiction for Jesus to be nonviolent and for God to bring about salvation through divinely orchestrated violence, through a scheme in which justice depended on violent retribution."[34] Weaver discards all contemporary reworkings of this model because they all depend on God-induced violence. He writes, "No amount of nuancing and redefining and reemphasizing this or that element will rescue satisfaction atonement from its intrinsically violent orientation, and from the image of God as the ultimate agent behind the death that satisfies God."[35] Thus, Weaver first rejects the satisfaction model because of its dependence on the violence of God.

Second, Weaver finds the satisfaction model to be problematic because it is not dependent upon the narrative of Jesus' life and ministry. The theory's action takes place outside of human history on some cosmic plane. He writes, "The formulation of satisfaction atonement theory allows persons to confess Christ for salvation, while unhooking ethics and ecclesiology from the particular ethic of Jesus."[36] Satisfaction theory

---

34. Weaver, *Nonviolent Atonement*, 204.

35. Ibid., "Narrative *Christus Victor*," 14.

36. Ibid., *Keeping Salvation Ethical*, 65.

separates atonement from ethics and discipleship in that it envisions a change in the believer's status beyond this life, but not a fundamental transformation or reorientation of the Christian's life.[37] It does not call attention to the need for radical discipleship, or point to the narrative of Jesus' life and teachings as a model for that discipleship.

The third problem with the satisfaction model, according to Weaver, is that it has no place for the resurrection. This model lacks the proleptic presence of the reign of God via resurrection. Therefore, it lacks any impulse toward confrontation with and witness to the social order. Instead, it tends to support the status quo.[38] Weaver agrees with feminist critiques of the satisfaction model's perpetuation the myth of redemptive suffering. He finds that this model poses an image of submission to oppression (through the victimization of Jesus) that obviously does not confront or challenge the actions of those who oppress and exploit.[39] In this way too, the satisfaction model separates cosmic (forensic) salvation from the life of Jesus, a life that Weaver believes constantly confronts the social status quo in order to reveal the inbreaking of the reign of God.

For these reasons, Weaver argues that satisfaction theory cannot be rehabilitated; it must be completely abandoned.[40] In its place, he picks up elements of the classical *Christus Victor* theory, but finds that the classical model contains some problematic elements, especially for contemporary believers. The classical model depicts a confrontation between God and the devil. Weaver believes that this model is not appropriate for contemporary Christians who no longer believe in personified evil or a personal devil. Also, Weaver argues that the classical model depends on a confrontation between the church (as an agent of God) and the world (which embraces the ways of the devil). He contends that contemporary believers no longer recognize this difference between the church and the world. Before the church aligned with the Roman Empire—the marriage of church and state—the beleaguered church represented the reign of God over against the world. After this shift, "the church no longer confronted empire and society; instead the church supported and was supported—established—by the empire."[41] Whereas early Christians be-

---

37. Ibid., "Narrative *Christus Victor*," 9; and ibid., *Keeping Salvation Ethical*, 47.

38. Ibid., *Nonviolent Atonement*, 54–55.

39. Ibid., "Narrative *Christus Victor*," 11.

40. Ibid., 2.

41. Ibid., *Nonviolent Atonement*, 83. Weaver adds that in the Constantinian shift, ethics changed from asking "how can we live within the story of Jesus" to "what must

lieved that the church represented the way of Jesus over against the world, contemporary believers often perceive that the world works the way it does because God has ordered it to be so. Weaver argues that this fundamental change in how Christians view the relationship between God and the world makes the classical model of *Christus Victor* inconceivable to contemporary believers who embrace the notion of a Christian nation or state.[42]

Another problem with the classical model is that it too (along with satisfaction theory) places the drama of salvation outside the realm of human history. It is not tied to the narrative of Jesus' life and ministry, nor does it demand discipleship from believers.

To solve the problems he finds in the classical *Christus Victor* model, Weaver proposes what he calls narrative *Christus Victor*.[43] This model essentially historicizes the drama of salvation. Weaver argues that the most distinctive feature of narrative *Christus Victor* is that it "put[s] the 'devil' back in atonement."[44] The object of Jesus' atoning death in the classical *Christus Victor* and ransom models is the devil. However, when Anselm removed the devil from this equation (because he could not abide the thought that the devil had certain rights that even God must respect), he made God the object of Jesus' atoning death. As we have noted, Weaver rejects the notion that God would demand Jesus' death in order to reconcile humanity to Godself. He argues that Jesus' death resulted from his confrontation with evil, not from a need to assuage God's wrath or desire for justice. Weaver emphasizes that this confrontation with evil takes place in history. He argues that evil powers exist in the sphere of human history, not just in the cosmic realm. In this way, he echoes Yoder's insistence that the powers continue to operate in and influence the world. For Weaver, "The devil or Satan is the name for the locus of all power that does not recognize the rule of God."[45] In other words, these powers are

be done to preserve the social order" (ibid., *Keeping Salvation Ethical*, 46).

42. The belief that the church is distinct and separated from the world (a two-kingdom theology), along with the corollary that the church became corrupted when it aligned with the world in the fourth century, is a recurring theme in Anabaptist theology. See, for example, Snyder, *Anabaptist History and Theology*, 114–15, 273; Yoder, *Royal Priesthood*, 54–64; and Friedmann, *Theology of Anabaptism*, 36–46.

43. Weaver, *Nonviolent Atonement*, 12–53.

44. Ibid., 308. This passage is taken from the second edition.

45. Ibid., 211. Weaver acknowledges that he draws on Walter Wink's understanding of the Powers here.

the accumulation of earthly structures that are organized into a system of domination that oppress and marginalize groups of people. In Weaver's model, then, the conflict between good and evil (or between God and Satan) takes place on earth between those who represent the reign of God (Jesus and the church) and those powers and systems of the world that do not recognize God's reign. Weaver believes that an earthly confrontation between groups of people with different allegiances makes more sense to contemporary believers than does an otherworldly battle between God and a personal devil.

To legitimate this historicization, Weaver examines the Revelation of John and concludes that it actually describes an earthly conflict (between the followers of Jesus and Rome) rather than a cosmic battle. He writes, "With the first-century context [of Revelation] in mind, it is clear that the symbolism of conflict and victory of the reign of God over the rule of Satan is a way of ascribing cosmic significance to the church's confrontation of the Roman empire in the first century."[46] Similarly, "these various symbolic images [in Revelation] have real historical antecedents and represent the institutions and the sources of power and authority that are followed by those who do not acknowledge the rule of God."[47] That is, the symbolism of Revelation provides a cosmic dimension to a very earthly confrontation between those who live under the reign of God and those who do not.

Weaver finds this same earthly confrontation in the gospel accounts. He argues that Jesus' mission was to make the reign of God present in the world.[48] Therefore, his entire life and ministry reflect the clash between the reign of God and those who oppose that reign:

> When the life of Jesus is understood as making the reign of God present in the historical realm, then the story of Jesus fits within a historicized version of *Christus Victor*. The motif appears clearly in the narrative of the temptation of Jesus in the wilderness. One may understand the account as an actual conversation of Jesus and Satan or as a metaphorical description of the kinds of temptations that could divert Jesus' mission. In either case, the story concerns the reign of God present in Jesus. That reign

46. Ibid., 27.

47. Ibid., 29.

48. Ibid., 58.

contrasts with and confronts the structures of the world which oppose the reign of God.[49]

Weaver stresses this historical, earthly confrontation between good and evil because this is how he makes sense of Jesus' death. He is quite clear that Jesus' death is not necessary to accomplish our salvation. Rather, it was the evil powers of the world (Satan, Rome, the powers of sin and death, etc.) that killed Jesus. He writes, "Neither the purpose nor the culmination of the mission was to die. God did not send Jesus to die, but to live, to make visible and present the reign of God."[50] Similarly, "the Son is carrying out the Father's will by making the reign of God visible in the world—and that mission is so threatening to the world that sinful human beings and that accumulation of evil they represent conspire to kill Jesus. Jesus came not to die, but to live, to witness to the reign of God in human history."[51] Weaver is quite clear that the impetus for the evil that killed Jesus came from the evil powers of the world, not from God.[52]

Just as Jesus' life and ministry reveal the nonviolent nature of God and God's reign, so too does Jesus' nonresistant submission to the powers that killed him. When he submitted to the evil powers that killed him (instead of meeting them on their own terms), he revealed that the reign of God does not depend on violence. Weaver argues that if Jesus had saved his own life through violent means, he would have abandoned his life-bringing and life-affirming mission.[53] Such an action would have undermined his entire mission to make present the nonviolent reign of God and thus negated his entire message. To remain true to God's nature and God's kingdom ethics, Jesus remained nonresistant and nonviolent to his death. In this way, Jesus' death was not the compensatory retribution for human sin. Rather, it was the logical result of his living out the reign of God.[54]

49. Ibid., *Keeping Salvation Ethical*, 39. He also notes that Jesus' programmatic announcement in Luke 4:14–30 proclaims that he represents the reign of God in history, which challenges the forces that enslave, whether economic or political. Jesus' acts of healing on the Sabbath and his encounters with women and foreigners are also efforts to make the reign of God visible over against the rule of evil in the social order (ibid., *Nonviolent Atonement*, 34, 38).

50. Ibid., 74.

51. Ibid., 211.

52. Ibid., 154.

53. Ibid., "Narrative *Christus Victor*," 25.

54. Ibid., *Nonviolent Atonement*, 42.

Weaver's model does not necessitate the death of Jesus, but it does emphasize the resurrection.[55] The resurrection is the victory described by the name *Christus Victor*. In the resurrection, God has defeated the powers that resist the divine reign. Despite the powers' best efforts, that reign is already breaking into human history. As Weaver explains, "With the resurrection of Jesus is revealed the true nature of reality, the universal rule of God . . . With the resurrection of Jesus, the future reign of God has already begun in human history. While the culmination still awaits, a piece of the future exists now."[56] The resurrection is also God's nonviolent way of vindicating Jesus' nonviolent and nonresistant life and ministry.[57] Weaver writes, "Resurrection is God's testimony that in Jesus is an advance sample of the reign of God that will become visible in its fullness when Jesus returns. To see the life and teaching of Jesus is to see how things are under the rule of God."[58]

Although evil will still be present in the world until the eschaton, followers of Jesus are called live into the reign of God here and now: "The eschatological element of narrative *Christus Victor* is an evangelical call to believe that Jesus represents the rule of God and to believe in the resurrection strongly enough to live in the presence of the reign of God *now*."[59] In other words, Christian discipleship is characterized by living in the reign of God as revealed by Jesus' life and validated by his resurrection. Weaver argues that "when the sinner is 'saved,' he or she changes loyalty from the rule of evil to the reign of God by accepting the call of God to new life in the reign of God. It is not a mere change of legal status before God, but a change in character and allegiance that means nothing—in fact, has not occurred—if there is no life lived according to the reign of God."[60] Similarly, "to be saved means to be located within the narrative of Jesus and to have a life shaped by that story."[61] Weaver acknowledges that following or imitating Jesus' example in this way may be costly to his disciples. It may entail suffering or even death as they

---

55. Of course this raises the question: If the model hinges on the resurrection, does it not first require Jesus to die?

56. Ibid., *Nonviolent Atonement*, 22.

57. Weaver points out that the ultimate victory over evil—the resurrection of Jesus—is nonviolent (ibid., 21).

58. Ibid., 40.

59. Ibid., 214, emphasis in original.

60. Ibid., 79–80.

61. Ibid., *Keeping Salvation Ethical*, 46.

confront the powerful systems and structures of this world. However, in Weaver's view that suffering is not itself salvific; it is a by-product of opposing evil, the price for beginning to resist.[62]

Although Weaver stresses that salvation does not actually occur until the Christian takes up a life of discipleship and lives according to the reign of God, he insists that his narrative *Christus Victor* model is not subjective. The resurrection reveals the true balance of power in the universe, whether or not anyone perceives it, for "In narrative *Christus Victor* the fundamental orientation of power in the universe has been altered . . . The reign of God is thus established whether or not any of us choose to submit to it."[63]

Weaver's narrative *Christus Victor* model thus upholds the nonviolent nature of God, is tied to the life and ministry of Jesus, and demands a life of discipleship from the believer. In these ways, Weaver addresses the problems he found in the satisfaction theories as well as the classical *Christus Victor* model. He has also constructed a model that maintains the core elements of the earliest Anabaptist writers.

There is much to appreciate in Weaver's model. First, he is adamant that salvation is not a matter of individual souls. While he claims that earthly resistance to the evil structures of the world has a counterpart in the cosmic realm, the focus of salvation is clearly in this world, as a part of human history. He writes, "For those who understand salvation within the framework of the victorious Christ who makes present the reign of God, salvation inherently includes saved relationships and structures as well as individuals."[64] This is not to deny the salvation of individuals, but rather to emphasize that the victory of God in Christ encompasses evil at all levels, from the personal and subjective to the powers and principalities of the cosmos.[65] It means that God's act of salvation is bigger than just the salvation of individuals; it has implications for the whole of society—at its socio-political level as well as the cosmic level.

---

62. Ibid., *Nonviolent Atonement*, 222, 174. This is Weaver's answer to feminist critiques that Jesus' nonresistance to his suffering on the cross creates a model that condones and even encourages unjust suffering for contemporary Christians, especially women. He argues that the Jesus depicted in narrative *Christus Victor* is not a passive victim. He actively confronts evil throughout his life, and thus becomes a model for our active confrontation of injustice and evil (ibid., 212, 174).

63. Ibid., 147, 154, 45.

64. Ibid., "Christus Victor, Ecclesiology," 288.

65. Ibid., "Some Theological Implications," 487.

Second, narrative *Christus Victor* makes good use of the biblical narrative of Jesus' life and ministry. Without the narrative of that life and ministry, we would not have an idea of what the reign of God looks like or how we should work toward its fulfillment. It is through Jesus' interactions with others—his inclusion of outsiders and the way he refused to return violence for violence, even in his death—that we catch a glimpse of how we must act in order to be part of the reign of God on earth.[66]

Third, Weaver provides a substantial role for the believer. In his model, the Christian does not just sit back and believe that his or her soul will be safe in heaven. Instead, the Christian has a responsibility to seek a transformation of his or her own life and also to work for the transformation of the world.

Despite these overwhelmingly positive aspects of Weaver's theory, some problems remain. Weaver is quite clear that Jesus did not come to die, and he claims that his atonement model does not require the death of Jesus. He is explicit in saying that neither God nor the reign of God needs Jesus' death. However, he writes in another essay that "without resurrection there is no salvation."[67] It may seem a trivial point, but if narrative *Christus Victor* model hinges on the resurrection, then it seems that his model *does* require Jesus to die. As critic Peter Martens points out, "How can God resurrect someone who is not dead?"[68] Granted, the way that

66. Weaver argues that the biblical narrative is crucial for Christian ethics because the creeds alone do not give us an ethical foundation: "If all we know of Jesus is that he is 'one substance with the Father' and that he is 'fully God and fully man,' there is nothing there that expresses the ethical dimension of being Christ-related, nothing there that would shape the church so that it can be a witness to the world" (ibid., *Nonviolent Atonement*, 93). See also ibid., "Christus Victor, Ecclesiology," 286–88.

67. Ibid., 288.

68. Martens, "Quest for an Anabaptist Atonement," 299. Although I agree with Martens on this point, I find his overall argument unconvincing. His claim that Jesus is not a victim because he *willingly* suffered a violent death is tenuous at best. Just because a spouse or child willingly endures domestic abuse to avoid sending a loved one to prison, or because a conscientious objector willingly endures torture and possibly death rather than recant his religious convictions, it does not mean that these people are not victims. Martens' insistence that Jesus voluntarily surrenders to death does not answer feminist and womanist contentions that Jesus' death can be considered divine child abuse.

Christopher Marshall's argument that Jesus had to die in order to stop the cycle of retributive violence is more convincing. He argues that by refusing to retaliate or defend himself, "Jesus broke the mimetic or pay-back mechanism that lies at the heart of sin's power" (Marshall, "Atonement, Violence," 91). Marshall adds, "The only way to achieve our salvation was for Jesus to tread the path of suffering and death, for only

narrative *Christus Victor* necessitates Jesus' death—either to depict the confrontation between the reign of God and the world or to validate Jesus' way of life and show God's power in the resurrection—is different, and in many ways preferable, to the way satisfaction or penal substitution theory necessitates his death by gruesome execution to satisfy God's justice or to assuage God's anger. Under Weaver's model, Jesus' death does not fulfill a need within God, as the other theories do. However, the fact that this model requires Jesus' death, for whatever reason, implies that for Weaver, God accomplished something in Jesus' death and resurrection that was not possible solely through Jesus' life and ministry.[69]

Although Weaver's model addresses—and fixes—some of the problems inherent in the classical *Christus Victor* theory, some complications remain. First, as we discussed in the critique of the original theory, it is difficult to believe that a victory has truly been won over the powers of evil when so many atrocious acts are committed every day and when vast numbers of people remain trapped in oppressive systems. Weaver acknowledges that evil will continue to act in the world, even after this ultimate victory, but believers are encouraged to seek comfort in the knowledge that victory lies with the rule of God.[70] Nevertheless, this explanation seems rather inadequate and not like a true victory at all.

Weaver is adamant that although his model continues to imagine Christ as a victor, his theory is thoroughly nonviolent. One of the strengths of Weaver's narrative *Christus Victor* model is that it acknowledges that the powers and principalities have a human face as well as a larger, cosmological character. As such, then, would those powers not also be subject to the cycle of retributive violence? Christopher Marshall writes that for many victims, retributive violence often seems to be the only way to appease the pain they have suffered and the resentment they feel.[71] It may be difficult to think of the powers of evil as victims of God's

---

thus could sin's power be broken" (ibid., 90). However, to say that God willed Jesus' death (in order to break the cycle of retributive violence or otherwise) because it was only way God could achieve our salvation seems a bit short-sighted, for such an argument severely limits the power and imagination of God.

69. This also raises the question of exactly what God accomplishes in the resurrection. Does it change something in the universe, or simply reveal that God has been in charge all along? For a complete discussion of this point, see Eisenbise, "Resurrection as Victory?" 16–17.

70. Weaver, "Reading the Past," 104–105.

71. Marshall, "Atonement, Violence," 90. Marshall is of course describing the cycle of *human* retributive violence and the power of sin and violence to turn those who

victory, but it seems that at least the human facet of those powers and principalities would almost certainly be affected by such feelings of pain and resentment. Would a defeat at the hands of God not push them to more drastic measures to try to gain victory over the reign of God? And even if we claim, as Weaver does, that this was the final defeat of the powers (and that they no longer have the ability to try more drastic measures), the metaphor of Christ the Victor is still shown to rest on power and might when Weaver highlights that God works through *weakness* to confront strength.[72]

The third problem with the victory-defeat motif is that it does not reflect the character of Jesus' ministry. The whole notion of Christian victory seems a bit odd, especially because winning never seemed to be a part of Jesus' mission and ministry. Instead, Jesus' mission was characterized by restoration (and restorative justice) rather than victory. In Jesus' human interactions, he did not emphasize defeat of his adversaries. Rather, he restored the powerless and marginalized back to some sort of place in society. In what is known as the programmatic statements of Jesus' ministry (Luke 4:18–19), Jesus describes his mission in terms of releasing the captives, restoring sight to the blind, and delivering the oppressed. Again and again we see in the gospel narratives of Jesus' life that he is working at restoration of what has been lost. From the hemorrhaging woman and the Gerasene demoniac, to the resurrection of Lazarus and the many acts of healing, Jesus is more concerned with restoration than with victory.

On the whole, Weaver's model is quite commendable. It addresses many of the problems with the *Christus Victor* theory and proposes a model of atonement that maintains emphases important to those in the Anabaptist tradition. But there are yet other Anabaptist theologians who propose different models.

C. Norman Kraus

C. Norman Kraus does not focus as exclusively on soteriology as Weaver does, but he too has developed a model of atonement that emphasizes

---

have been sinned against into sinners in their own right. However, it seems that the powers of evil in the world would be even more likely to turn toward retributive violence when their efforts have been thwarted.

72. See Weaver, "Some Theological Implications," 490–91.

certain core Anabaptist beliefs. Kraus' theology generally reflects a characteristically Anabaptist Christocentrism. He argues that "the historical revelation in Jesus remains the norm for defining the authentic Christ image and the Christian's experience of God."[73] Thus, along with Weaver, Kraus emphasizes that an adequate explanation of Jesus' cross should be historically based and contain the challenge of Jesus' life and mission for present-day disciples.

Kraus' model is also nonviolent. He claims that the mainline Protestant tradition has interpreted the cross in a way that justifies imperialism and the use of violence to attain God's kingdom. Kraus proposes a different model: "This is a 'peace theology' in the Anabaptist tradition. For many years it has seemed to me that the biblical peace position does not fit well on the traditional Protestant theological foundation. What is needed is a more comprehensive theological perspective that will undergird and more consistently explain the implications of the cross and resurrection as God's way of dealing with evil."[74] That is, Kraus recognizes the need for a nonviolent theory of atonement that stresses peace and justice as the way of Jesus and of God.

Like Weaver, Kraus rejects the notion that God somehow demanded Jesus' death. Kraus writes, "The cross involved no equivalent compensation or payment of penalty demanded by God's anger. God is justified in forgiving us on the basis of his own holy love and not on the basis of an equivalent penal satisfaction which has been paid to him through the death of Jesus."[75] He argues that revelation in Jesus shows that God is pure holy love or grace, not a mixture of love and some other characteristic, such as justice.[76]

---

73. Kraus, *Jesus Christ Our Lord*, 25. However, the risen Christ is also crucial to Kraus' theology. He also uses the composite of the apostolic witness about the crucified and risen Lord as another criteria for theological interpretation (ibid., 17–18).

74. Ibid., 17.

75. Ibid., 225.

76. Ibid., *God Our Savior*, 52. He adds that God is radically opposed to evil and that righteousness in the face of evil is actually one of the dimensions of God's love. However, this does not mean that God's love is bound or constrained by any law of justice (ibid., *Jesus Christ Our Lord*, 87). Similarly, "We must speak of God's wrath as an aspect of his love, not as a separate characteristic in paradoxical contrast to his love. God's love is holy. It is inexorably opposed to sin and evil. As strange as it may sound, we must say that God's wrath is the anguish and indignation of God's love confronting evil and its consequences" (ibid., *God Our Savior*, 100–101).

According to Kraus, traditional Trinitarian theology has conceptualized Christ in terms of the eternal Trinity, instead of allowing its notion of God or the Godhead to be informed by the actions of the Jesus: "The result is that the ethical character of God remains somehow different from and often inconsistent with the picture of God the Son dying on the cross. *Agape* as revealed in Jesus is carefully circumscribed by the justice of the eternal Trinity."[77] In other words, traditional Protestant theology is more concerned with explaining Jesus' actions (or death) in terms of some outside understanding of God's justice than with examining the actions of Jesus to determine what they reveal about God's nature. Kraus denies that God's nature is somehow different than that which is revealed by Jesus.[78] Jesus' actions are intimately linked with God's nature. The incarnation shows how God is at work in the way Jesus himself was at work. Indeed, Kraus does not attribute Christ's deity to his pre-existence or his divine attributes, but rather to the identification of the word spoken (or lived) by Jesus with the eternal Word.[79] Kraus writes, "When we speak of Christ as deity we are not saying that Jesus is a god or divine man like the Creator and Judge who has revealed himself in nature and Law. Rather, we are saying that God is the kind of God who relates to the universe, human beings, and history like he related to us in Christ."[80] In this way, Kraus' picture of God is directly shaped by Jesus' human actions. In fact, Kraus stresses Jesus' human actions to the point that he locates the beginning of salvation in Jesus' earthly life. As Kraus explains, "His salvation activity as the Messiah was already begun in his earthly ministry. We need not wait for his death on the cross to begin to speak of salvation or the saving work of Christ."[81] However, Kraus does find meaning in the cross, but this meaning differs from most Protestant theology. Kraus'

---

77. Ibid., *Jesus Christ Our Lord*, 113–14.

78. However, Kraus claims that we do see God's wrath in Jesus' indignation and opposition to evil, as well as his resolute noncooperation with it by refusing to give it even the semblance of justification in his trial and crucifixion (ibid., *God Our Savior*, 211–12). Here, it becomes clear that Kraus' understanding of God is closer to Weaver's than to Holland's or Reimer's.

79. Ibid., 104. Although he rejects accusations of adoptionism, Kraus does downplay the pre-existence of Christ as well as his divinity (ibid., *Jesus Christ Our Lord*, 67, 103–105). Jesus' human actions are especially important for Kraus, but he maintains that these actions reveal God's nature.

80. Ibid., 103.

81. Ibid., 138.

unique contribution to atonement theology is his claim that Jesus' death on the cross liberates humanity from shame.

According to Kraus, human alienation from God has more to do with shame than with guilt. He contrasts the two concepts by explaining that guilt results from moral fault and is experienced as anticipation of deserved punishment, whereas shame has more to do with uncleanness or defilement.[82] Shame and guilt are further differentiated by how they affect communal relationships. Guilt can be expunged by punishment, and relationships can be restored once the victim feels compensated. Shame, by contrast, cannot be erased by compensation. The only means by which shame can be removed is to exclude the shamed one from the community. There is no ritual or punishment that can heal a relationship fractured by shame. Shame causes alienation, exclusion, and rage—all feelings that sever communication. Therefore, the only way to banish shame is to re-establish communication and reaffirm the worth of the shamed individual.[83] Kraus claims that this is exactly what Jesus accomplished on the cross.

The cross was an instrument of a very shameful death: "It was designed to be an instrument of contempt and public ridicule. The victim died naked, in a bloody sweat, helpless to control bodily excretions."[84] Death by crucifixion was designed to maximize the condemned's feelings of degradation and exclusion. Jesus endures this most shameful death in order to reveal that God identifies with us and our shame. As Kraus explains, "Jesus, whom they knew to be innocent, voluntarily became a victim of those powers that degraded and humiliated the masses. He did this in solidarity with them, representing their cause when he might have escaped."[85]

Thus, Jesus' death on the cross reveals his solidarity with us, but his resurrection shows God's solidarity with him—and with us. Jesus' resurrection reveals that God affirms the worth of the shamed one; God

---

82. Green and Baker, *Recovering the Scandal*, 155–57. Kraus is writing in the context of Japanese culture, which is considered to be a shame-based culture, in contrast to North American culture, which is often characterized by fault or blame, guilt, and retributive punishment (Kraus, *Jesus Our Lord*, 212–13). However, Green and Baker claim that Kraus' analysis, which is constructed around the problem of shame, is actually more closely connected to Jesus' world and the gospels' worldview.

83. Kraus, *Jesus Christ Our Lord*, 211.

84. Green and Baker, *Recovering the Scandal*, 163.

85. Kraus, *God Our Savior*, 35.

restores Jesus' dignity, and welcomes him back into relationship. As Kraus observes, "In this way he made the cross the liberating symbol for the oppressed. That he died with dignity and compassion even for his tormentors reversed the meaning of crucifixion. The cross, intended to be a symbol of failure and humiliation, became for believers the symbol of victory and new self identity."[86] The image of God sharing our existential shame allows us to emerge from self-isolation to confess our failures and to let go of our feelings of unworthiness and despair. In this way, the possibility of identifying with Jesus as a part of God's family is opened to us.[87] Consequently, Jesus' identification with the shamed ones allows us to realize a new self-identity as children of God.[88]

Shame cannot be erased by substitutionary compensation. Rather, only a forgiveness that includes a genuine restoration of relationship (and overcoming exclusion and alienation) can banish shame.[89] God's resurrection of Jesus, and therefore God's identification with and welcome to all those who have suffered shame, is how God heals the relationship with humanity:

> God is not ultimately interested in judgment which results in a perfect balance of retributive justice . . . God's ultimate goal is reconciliation, restoration of relationship, reintegration, and unification of the created order. Or to put it another way, God's goal is victory over the frustration, bondage, and death caused by sin. Salvation is not the gift of paradise, a gift detached from God himself. Salvation is a relationship to God.[90]

In other words, Jesus significantly changed the picture: "Through his passion and resurrection we are offered new possibilities for a quality of life and personal relationship here and now."[91] Christ did not come just to provide a means to forgive past sins or to teach a higher moral ideal. Instead, "He came actually to inaugurate a new beginning. The final

---

86. Ibid.

87. Ibid., *Jesus Christ Our Lord*, 220.

88. Green and Baker, *Recovering the Scandal*, 166.

89. Kraus, *Jesus Christ Our Lord*, 211.

90. Ibid., 168.

91. Ibid., 173. Kraus' model also contains a substitutionary piece. Because Jesus suffered the ultimate shameful exclusion by way of his crucifixion, we can be free from the fear of such exclusion (Green and Baker, *Recovering the Scandal*, 166).

purpose of God in Christ [was] . . . to create a new order of relationships in keeping with his own nature and will to love."[92]

In this way, then, Jesus reveals a new pattern of relationships in society. Indeed, "What the orthodox Protestant tradition has not seemed to recognize is that the changed pattern of relationships is an essential part of the gospel of salvation itself . . . Christ's salvation has been appropriated where this pattern of relationships is realized and to the extent that it is realized among us."[93] Living this changed pattern of relationships is another way of describing what other Anabaptists have called a life of radical discipleship. Solidarity with Christ includes the gift of the Spirit, or the attitude of Christ, along with the adoption of his lifestyle and participation in his mission.[94]

Solidarity with Christ also has a necessary social dimension. Salvation is a communal or social element; it is not just personal. Solidarity in Christ's mission does not exclude personal evangelism, "but the mission of Jesus as the Messiah dare not be restricted to the narrower definition of evangelism as calling individuals out of the world which has already been prejudged to damnation."[95] Salvation, or the kingdom (Kraus claims that the two are synonymous and cannot be contrasted), is expressed in terms of social actions and organized movements, as a social-spiritual possibility that is announced and inaugurated by following the style of Jesus' life, death, and resurrection.[96]

The church has a special role to play in witnessing to salvation or the coming kingdom, for as Kraus explains, "The congregation as a local community of salvation must demonstrate the new creation order in its own organized life as an integral part of the salvation message."[97] In other words, the community lives into the kingdom through its changed relationships. It becomes the location of the inbreaking kingdom. Thus, the church must give an authentic witness to Jesus' way of being in the world, because "Only as the church bears witness through its life to the

---

92. Ibid., 145.

93. Ibid., 241.

94. Ibid., 239.

95. Ibid., 244.

96. Kraus, *God Our Savior*, 179, 172; and ibid., *Jesus Christ Our Lord*, 140.

97. Ibid., *God Our Savior*, 179.

way of servanthood and the cross—in contrast to the political saviors of the world—can the true identity of Christ be known to the world."[98]

In some ways, Kraus' soteriological model differs significantly from Weaver's model. However, the two authors are similar in that they both reject the violence inherent in the satisfaction theory and propose models of atonement that contain three distinctive Anabaptist emphases we examined earlier in this essay: the nonviolent nature of God, the importance of the life and ministry of Jesus, and the need for discipleship as the human response to God's gift of salvation. But, in considering Kraus' theory, one is left to wonder whether Jesus' death had any objective effect on the world. Certainly there is value in recognizing Jesus' solidarity with shamed ones (and Kraus' theory taps into much of the recent scholarship exploring the great impact honor and shame had on first-century Mediterranean culture). Nevertheless, after analyzing Yoder's and Weaver's claims that Jesus' death—and especially his life—changed (or revealed) the balance of powers in the universe such that the powers of evil are now defeated, Kraus' understanding of the effect of Jesus' life and death seems fairly small: it makes our own shame easier to bear because Jesus was shamed too. Kraus argues that shame can only be overcome by a genuine restoration of relationship, but does not explain exactly how Jesus' shameful death and vindicating resurrection accomplishes that restoration. In a way, it seems that although Kraus' model gives individuals a way to cope with their own shame, it does not change the conditions of the world that led to that shame in the first place.

Sharon L. Baker

Sharon Baker's atonement model focuses on forgiveness and restorative justice. She argues that satisfaction theory has no room for true forgiveness. In the satisfaction theory, God receives recompense in form of satisfaction, which makes forgiveness unnecessary. Satisfaction is not forgiveness because "God receives something for someone before God forgives sin. The meaning of the word 'forgiveness' however, indicates a giving *before* receiving or even a giving without receiving, a sacrificial giving that *gives up* receiving any recompense at all."[99] Therefore, Baker

---

98. Ibid., 38.
99. Baker, "By Grace?" 135–36, emphasis in original.

prefers to use the term "fore-giveness" to stress that this is an absolution granted in advance, before a person repents or pays back.[100]

Just as satisfaction theory implies the wrong idea of forgiveness, it likewise contains a warped understanding of God's justice, according to Baker. Satisfaction theories depend on human ideas of retributive justice or punishment. Baker argues, however, that human justice and mercy are very different from divine justice and mercy: "Where human justice is retributive, quantitative, and destructive of relationships, God's justice is restorative, qualitative, and builds relationships."[101] Restorative justice forgives the crime and seeks to redeem wrongdoing by repairing relationships, in contrast to retributive justice, which seeks to control wrongdoing through punishment.

Baker's concept of divine, restorative justice precludes the idea that God would demand, desire, or will the passion and death of Jesus to forgive sin.[102] God did not demand punishment or retribution.[103] Instead, God displayed fore-giveness by answering Jesus' prayer from the cross.[104] As Baker explains, "Jesus' prayer for forgiveness from the cross summoned the compassion of God to transform the violence of human existence into compassion, love, and forgiveness. God's act of forgiveness reveals to humanity the true nature of divine justice as mercy, as restorative, and as reconciling."[105] In other words, Jesus' actions during his passion reveal the divine response to violence and injustice, for "Rather

100. Ibid., 139, n. 47.

101. Ibid.

102. Ibid., 131. However, Baker does argue (following Aquinas' ideas of God's providence) that God does will the passion, but only out of God's respect for human freedom. She writes, "Although I do not argue that God willed the violence inflicted upon the innocent man Jesus (in fact I argue the opposite), I do contend that God knew the violence would occur considering human freedom and sin, and yet at the same time knew that the divine plan would still be consummated in spite of human opposition through sin" (ibid., 120). In other words, God could have chosen another means of reconciliation, but the passion became necessary because human agents responded to Jesus with violence (ibid., 121).

103. In fact, Baker argues that Christ could have died a natural death and still remained obedient to God's will, giving his life for the salvation of all creation (ibid., 121). However, the meaning of this passage is not entirely clear. It seems that Baker means to say that Jesus devoted his life to reconciling relationships such that all of creation would experience salvation, although Baker's words could also be interpreted to say that Jesus gave up his life for the salvation of creation.

104. "Forgive them, for they know not what they do" (Luke 23:34).

105. Baker, "By Grace?" 165.

than shouting threats of retaliation in the name of God, Christ set in motion the ultimate expression of divine justice and its restorative character by asking God to forgive us."[106] Jesus sought the reverse of revenge: he prayed for the forgiveness of his killers. He stopped the cycle of retributive violence so that the great injustice of the cross resulted in compassionate reconciliation.[107]

God forgives before (and without) Jesus' satisfaction, but according to Baker, Jesus does make a sacrifice: "He sacrifices repayment for sin; he sacrificed his right to take his pound of flesh; he sacrificed receiving back (as God) what was owed by humanity for the offense of sin. Jesus Christ, therefore, offered us a sacrifice of cosmic proportion. He sacrificed repayment or satisfaction for the debt we owed and the punishment we deserved."[108] Instead of calling on God to avenge his death, Jesus forgoes his right to retributive justice. Instead, he asks for reconciling justice by asking God to forgive those who killed him.

Baker cannot call for a wholly nonviolent theory of atonement because the crucifixion was violent, and she does not seek to downplay the violence or suffering that Christ endured. Nonetheless, she finds that Jesus' actions throughout his life as well as his response to the crucifixion show that God is not only nonviolent, but "anti-violence."[109] The violence of the crucifixion, therefore, comes from humanity, not from God, and Baker argues that any adequate model of atonement must make that clear. She finds that the atonement models that attribute violence to the divine character end up perpetuating violence. In contrast, Baker's model stresses that the desire for violent retribution is human, not divine:

> Christ reveals to us that God's justice is mercy in the form of restoration, reconciliation, and redemption from the strong powers of the world. Where reconciliation is the focus, violence

106. Ibid., 144.

107. Ibid., 164.

108. Ibid., 159. This idea becomes a bit problematic when held in tension with the understanding that Jesus effects our salvation by asking God to forgive us. The idea of Jesus' sacrificing the payment owed to him clearly places him within the Godhead. This idea is echoed by Baker's claim that Christ "saves us 'simply by being God with us,' God in solidarity with us even in the midst of our worst pain and suffering" (ibid., 162). And yet, it seems that her model also includes the notion that Jesus effects our salvation by crying out on the cross, summoning God's compassion to forgive us. In the latter conception, Jesus' actions seem to affect God or change God's mind in much the same way as in the satisfaction theories.

109. Ibid., 167.

is cut short. Where restoration of relationships is foremost in theories of atonement, violence is precluded from the divine character. Where violence is seen as a human act free from any connection with God's way of acting or redeeming humanity, legitimate use of coercive power no longer holds sway over society, governments, or families.[110]

Baker argues that to be true followers of Jesus, Christians are also called to give up their notions of retributive justice and redemptive violence. Disciples are to follow Jesus' example in forgiving and reconciling relationships. Baker writes, "I believe that Christ's life, death, and resurrection not only reversed the human conception of retributive justice to conceptions of restorative and reconciling justice, but in so doing Jesus demonstrated how we are to negotiate our relationships with others, seeking reconciliation and restoration, peace, and justice rather than retribution through warfare or (governmental) terrorism."[111] Like Jesus, we are to absorb the cost of evil by forgiving it, by refusing to transmit it, by blocking it.[112] To do so is to live in the kingdom of God.

In summary, Baker's model hinges on the nonviolent, reconciling, and forgiving action of God and Jesus. She argues that Jesus' passion and death were caused by human action but that Jesus' reaction, in sacrificing his right for retribution and instead asking God to forgive us, reconciles us to God and to one another:

> In light of divine justice as restorative rather than retributive, then, Jesus' passion *does* satisfy; but it satisfies human justice rather than divine justice. It *is* punitive or penal, but it is human punishment for speaking the truth. Conversely, divine justice relinquishes retribution or satisfaction for sin in order to restore humanity's relationship with God, and simultaneously redeems humanity through the act of forgiveness.[113]

That Baker's model emphasizes that Jesus' death was caused by human action rather than by divine will is certainly one of its strengths. Her distinction between retributive and restorative justice is also helpful in that it highlights that God's ways are not human ways, and we should not expect them to be. Although it is admirable that Anselm wanted to

110. Ibid., 7.

111. Ibid., 163.

112. Ibid., 190.

113. Ibid., 143–44.

maintain God's justice in his satisfaction theory, it seems that his understanding of how God works was too narrow. His model anthropomorphizes God by expecting that God will be offended by a particular situation simply because that is how humans would react in that situation. Baker's model allows for a more creative God, one who reacts in imaginative and unexpected ways.

It is also admirable that Baker does not downplay the violence of the crucifixion even though her model maintains that neither God nor Jesus is violent. In this way, her model takes the power of evil seriously by confronting the horrific actions humans perpetrate on one another. The problem, however, is that although Baker claims that God did not demand Jesus' death, it seems that perhaps her model does. If Jesus' saving action is his unexpected reaction to his murder, then that makes his death necessary. To be sure, Baker also finds that Jesus exemplified God's restorative justice throughout his life, but she seems to suggest that his death provided the greatest opportunity for Jesus to display God's variety of justice.

Joel B. Green and Mark D. Baker

Like the authors we have already studied, Joel Green and Mark Baker find elements of the satisfaction theory of atonement problematic. They argue that even though this has become the most popular theory, especially in America,[114] it is not the only explanation of the salvific nature of Jesus' death. Indeed, they find that the New Testament offers several different themes that address Jesus' atoning death:

---

114. Like Sharon Baker, Joel Green and Mark Baker argue that satisfaction theory is based on retributive justice or punishment, and that this theory is agreeable to Americans because we are steeped in this particular view of justice through our own system of criminal justice, which focuses on determining fault and meting out punishment: "A world where this system of justice has reached the stage of 'the way the world works' or 'the way the world really is' or even 'the way the world was made by God' is naturally receptive to a theory of atonement like that provided in penal substitution. Indeed, to suggest that such a theory is limited, or only a theory, or even inadequate in light of the biblical witness would be to call into question a central aspect of the world that most of us take for granted" (Green and Baker, *Recovering the Scandal*, 24). Similarly, they argue that penal substitution fits American individualism. American society tends to think of people as autonomous actors who commit wrongdoings because of their own faults rather than because they are embedded within social systems. Individual justification by faith therefore makes sense in such a context (ibid., 25).

1) Humanity does not have the wherewithal to save itself, but instead needs help from God.

2) There is a necessary human response to God's gracious gift, for "We are saved *from*, it is true, but we are also saved *for* . . . Atonement *theology* cannot be separated from *ethics*."

3) God was somehow at work in the cross for human salvation.

4) What happened on the cross was of universal significance. It does not privilege one group over another.[115]

Green and Baker combine these themes to propose a model of atonement that interprets salvation as status reversal. The gospel accounts consistently depict Jesus interacting with those on the underside of society and criticizing those in power. In fact, Green and Baker argue that Jesus' life and his upside-down kingdom ethics undermined the whole cultural system in which he lived. Jesus rejected the Roman system of patronage and special privilege, he argued that the kingdom of God belonged to children and those who had absolutely no status in the world, and he rejected all notions of debt and reciprocal obligation. As Green and Baker conclude, "Jesus' message thus crossed the grain of the Roman political order not only at the level of practice and attitudes but also with respect to the most basic questions about 'how the world works.'"[116]

These authors even find support for their model of atonement as status reversal in the ransom sayings (Mark 10:45; 14:24), passages that are usually seen as the clearest scriptural proof for satisfaction theory or substitutionary atonement. They argue that the narrative placement of these two passages is important: "The points at which a theology of atonement is most transparent in the Gospel tradition are intimately related to scenes where the sorts of concerns with power- and status-seeking characteristic of the Roman Empire are on display among Jesus' followers."[117] The narrative context for the ransom saying in Mark and its parallel in Matthew is the sons of Zebedee requesting the primary seats of honor in the kingdom banquet (Mark 10:45; Matt 20:28). Jesus thus contrasts his own life and mission (to give his life for many) with his disciples' status-seeking behavior. As Green and Baker explain, "In other words, Jesus' death demonstrates the distance between God's ways and

115. Ibid., 112–13, emphasis in original.

116. Ibid., 40.

117. Ibid., 39.

the ways of typical human communities. Top-down relations of power, social obligations, struggling for honor and recognition—these patterns of behavior are opposed by the cross at the most basic level."[118]

The same status-seeking behavior forms the context for the Last Supper tradition, which stems from the disciples squabbling over their relative greatness (Luke 22:7–38). Green and Baker observe, "Again, then, Jesus' representation of the atoning sacrifice of his impending death is set in a context in which it provides a stark alternative to the world system to which his followers continually fall prey."[119]

Thus, Jesus' life and death were not about cosmic satisfaction. Instead, his life and death were about instigating a new order in the world, an order by which the lowly will be elevated. The authors explain: "In his suffering and resurrection, Jesus embodied the fullness of salvation interpreted as status reversal; his death was the center point of the divine-human struggle over how life is to be lived, in humility or self-glorification . . . In his death, and in consequence of his resurrection by God, the way of salvation is exemplified and made accessible to all those who will follow."[120]

Like Weaver, Green and Baker claim that Jesus' death was the result of his mission. Undermining the power structures and the whole cultural system of his time led to Jesus' crucifixion. However, in Jesus' resurrection, God vindicates the life that Jesus led by reversing Jesus' status from the humiliated one to the exalted one. Indeed, "It was precisely in his humiliation and exaltation that Jesus exemplified the nature of salvation and made salvation available for those of 'humble circumstances'—the hungry, the powerless, the lost, the marginal. Jesus' death thus occupied the central ground in the divine-human struggle over how life is to be lived, whether in humility or self-glorification."[121]

In this way, Jesus' life and death both reveal how we are to live. Therefore, discipleship, or living Jesus' way of life, is an integral part of the atonement model Green and Baker propose.[122] Living as Christian

118. Ibid.

119. Ibid., 43.

120. Ibid., 77.

121. Ibid., 14. James McClendon echoes this idea. He writes, "God reversed all human judgment by identifying the life of Jesus of Nazareth afresh with God's own life" at the resurrection (McClendon, *Doctrine*, 247).

122. They argue that satisfaction theories tend to obscure Jesus' words that his disciples are supposed to pick up and carry their own crosses. Instead of Jesus' suffering

disciples means modeling our own behavior and way of life on the actions of Jesus, the humble and humiliated one. It means living out an ethic characterized by status reversal. It means living no longer for oneself, but for Christ—and thus, for others.[123] However, those who live out the values of the kingdom of God will most likely be met with resistance from the world, just as Jesus was. This is because "Those whose lives are unreservedly oriented toward the purpose of God in a world that has set itself over against that purpose can expect little else."[124] And yet, we are still called to pick up our crosses and follow Jesus.

Like the other models examined in this chapter, Green and Baker's model has several important advantages. It highlights that Jesus' death was a result of the way he lived, not the will of God. It also provides an active role for the believer, stressing that a life of discipleship is a crucial part of salvation. We might classify this model as a revamped *Christus Victor* theory insofar as it argues that Jesus' resurrection vindicates his way of living and exalts him (and thus gives him victory) over the powers that humiliated him. Many of the models in this chapter underscore the importance of the resurrection as a sort of divine stamp of approval on the way Jesus lived his life. This idea is certainly appealing, for it affirms that God did not will Jesus' death, yet still constructed something positive out of it, and also that God's ways are the nonviolent ways of Jesus. Though this model does not necessarily require a physical, bodily resurrection, the question remains as to whether or not the resurrection has the same vindicating effect if it is metaphorical rather than literal or historical. This question may be problematic for some contemporary Christians whose worldview does not include the possibility of the resurrection as a resuscitated body.

Thomas N. Finger

Thomas Finger picks up many of the themes of the writers we have already discussed. Like the other Anabaptist theologians discussed here, Finger rejects the notion that God or the law of God's justice demanded Jesus' death, but he argues that Jesus "had to die" because that is the way

---

becoming exemplary, penal substitution makes it *for us* (Green and Baker, *Recovering the Scandal*, 27).

123. Ibid., 59.

124. Ibid., 26–27.

God's love operates in the face of evil.[125] Like Weaver, Finger acknowledges that there are powers at work in the world that reject the reign of God and hold sway over humanity. Like others before him, Finger acknowledges that suffering is a likely consequence of the mission of Jesus and his disciples:

> It is the powers, ranged over against God, who inflict the death penalty although Jesus was innocent. God does not inflict such a penalty, save in the indirect sense of allowing it to be exacted, without intervening violently to prevent it, because this was an inevitable consequence of their mission of self-sacrificing love.[126]

Thus, Jesus did not pay a price demanded by God. In fact, Finger argues that the early Anabaptists did not use the language of justification as much as they talked about ontological transformation.[127] Finger uses the term "divinization" to describe this ontological transformation, and he defines it as participating inwardly and living outwardly in accord with Jesus' death and resurrection.[128] He stresses that divinization is not a transformation of human reality *into* divine reality, but rather the transformation *by* divine reality of those who remain fully human.[129] In other words, divinization means remaining human while being deeply transformed by God. In some ways, then, Finger's model is an Anabaptist reworking of Athanasius' theory.

Finger's notion of divinization contains both an objective and subjective element. The inward transformation is accomplished by God. Through faith, the Holy Spirit incorporates people into Christ's life, death, and resurrection.[130] Jesus' resurrection bestows the Spirit, which cleans out inner human corruption to clear the channel of poison, opening it to God:

> Jesus' nonviolent, servantlike humanity did not simply set an example, even a highly inspiring one. It was a Spirit-imbued

125. Finger, "*Christus Victor* as Nonviolent Atonement," 99.

126. Ibid., 99–100.

127. Ibid., *Contemporary Anabaptist Theology*, 137. Finger claims that Hubmaier believed that the main content of salvation was neither forgiveness nor righteousness, but rather ontological transformation.

128. Ibid., 151.

129. Ibid., 114.

130. Ibid., 129.

comportment through which Jesus resisted and countered the powers' domineering, violent energy. This spiritual energy alone, released at his resurrection, could dissolve the poison which that violent energy had spread through other people; it alone could rip up the roots of fear, aggression, and pride which that energy aroused and by which it had taken them captive.[131]

In addition to releasing this spiritual energy, Jesus' death accomplished something else for humanity. Jesus suffered his death alone, but because he has already endured this separation from God, humanity does not have to go through the process alone. Finger argues, "Jesus passed alone through the horror of final separation from God, but he was raised to life by his Father through the Spirit. Consequently, when people joined to the risen Jesus are dying, this one who was crucified accompanies them."[132] Similarly, Finger stresses that "Jesus passed through death, which is abandonment by God, which we all deserve, *alone*—and that consequently we need not. Why? Basically because when we pass through death, we will not be alone, for he will be with us."[133] Finger is quite clear that this aspect of salvation is accomplished by God. It is a compassionate gift for humanity, which suffers under death's dominion.

However, divinization is not just an inward process; whoever partakes of the divine character conforms to the image of Jesus in all submission, obedience, and righteousness.[134] In other words, Christians seek divinization by following and emulating Christ. Jesus' teaching and example are essential, for "They were intrinsic to his own path and to revealing and preparing the path that all humans must take to salvation. Jesus provided the 'structural model' for our lives."[135] But as Finger is careful to point out, this emphasis on the human aspect of this transformation does not set up unrealistic expectations that ignore human limitations because this ontological transformation is intrinsically patterned. Rather, "It reflect[s] Jesus' life, death, and resurrection—*christomorphically*. Divinization was shaped by—even as it reshaped—the finite world, including suffering and death. Anabaptists traveled this journey *inwardly*, through spiritual participation in Christ, and simultaneously

131. Ibid., 360.

132. Ibid., 362.

133. Ibid., "*Christus Victor* as Nonviolent Atonement," 105, emphasis in original.

134. Ibid., *Contemporary Anabaptist Theology*, 130.

135. Ibid., 359.

outwardly along the path through the material world opened by his life and death."[136]

Although Finger uses the Orthodox idea of divinization, his claim that there is an inner and an outer form of salvation clearly reflects elements of sixteenth-century Anabaptist theology. Like the early Anabaptists, Finger stresses that one cannot have an inward or spiritual experience of salvation or rebirth without a corresponding desire for a life of discipleship. In the same way, if one's outer life does not reflect a way of living patterned on Jesus' life and ministry, that person's inner or spiritual state should be questioned. However, Finger—and the early Anabaptists—also stress that salvation (or divinization) occurs as the gracious gift of God. God's actions through Jesus and in the heart of the believer make that life of discipleship possible. Indeed, "They could attempt discipleship because God's new creation was already present. They could endure terrible oppression and their own shortcomings because it was not yet fully present—yet they kept going because it surely would be."[137]

Finger's adherence to traditional elements of Anabaptist soteriology is admirable, and his work in weaving together those elements with some Orthodox understandings is compelling. However, according to his model, Jesus' death does not seem to have much impact on the Earth. If the whole of salvation is in not having to suffer death alone, does that make the point of Jesus' death and our own salvation an after-death reward? In his critique of this understanding of atonement, Jürgen Moltmann writes, "The death of Christ cannot only come to fruition in an existentialist interpretation, in the ability of the believer to die in peace, important though that may be."[138] For this reason, Finger's model does not seem very satisfying, especially in light of the other models discussed in this chapter that claim Jesus' life, ministry, death, and resurrection had an effect on the powers of this world. Thus, although Finger does highlight the need for Christians to live out lives of discipleship that could potentially have an effect on this world, his model seems to place too much emphasis on the benefits salvation provides upon our own deaths.

136. Ibid., 131–32, emphasis in original.
137. Ibid., 145.
138. Moltmann, *Crucified God*, 217.

Mary H. Schertz

As we have seen, many Anabaptist theologians emphasize the necessity of discipleship and also embrace, or at least acknowledge and accept, the suffering that may come from the world's reaction to that discipleship. In this way, it may appear that they valorize suffering and find it redemptive. In fact, some early Anabaptists believed that a person's faith is not true faith until it has been tested.[139] However, most contemporary Anabaptist theologians are sensitive to feminist critiques of redemptive suffering and would argue that although suffering may result from following the path of discipleship that plays an integral role in salvation, suffering itself is not salvific. Mary Schertz offers just such an argument.

Based on her analysis of Luke's gospel, Schertz begins her argument with the claim that Jesus' suffering and death are not redemptive. She argues that Luke neither glorifies suffering nor reduces salvation to the cross. Instead, "the suffering and death of Jesus is salvific because in suffering and dying Jesus held true to the nonviolent kingdom of God that he lived to proclaim and enact."[140] She argues that in carrying out his mission to proclaim the kingdom of God, Jesus endangered himself: "He put himself into peril and suffered the consequences of those decisions. In that sense, the tragedy of the cross was inevitable."[141] In this way, Schertz echoes the argument of all the writers we have studied by pointing out that Jesus' death was the result of the world's negative reaction to his life and mission, not the result of God's desire for satisfaction or punishment.

Jesus' death was inevitable because of the nature of the reign he proclaimed, but it is not his death alone that is salvific. His death is important (and even salvific), but only because it is a part of how Jesus proclaimed and enacted the reign of God. As Schertz affirms:

> The suffering of Jesus on the cross is an integral part of that proclamation and enactment, but it does not define redemption . . . What is redemptive is the kingdom of God. People are saved and their sins are erased or blotted out when they stop resisting the kingdom and become, in turn, proclaimers and enactors of this kingdom. The conversion of individuals is possible because Jesus preached, taught, healed, exorcised demons, suffered, died, and was raised–all to announce and bring about the kingdom of

139. See, for example, Friedmann, *Theology of Anabaptism*, 84.

140. Schertz, "God's Cross and Women's Questions," 206.

141. Ibid., 202.

God. Conversion of individuals comes through the Holy Spirit
and the faithfulness of believers who continue to proclaim and
enact the kingdom of God in the name of Jesus.[142]

Schertz acknowledges that proclaiming and enacting the kingdom
may be just as dangerous for Jesus' followers as it was for him. However,
she argues that Jesus' words to his followers about taking up their crosses
and following him does not contain the language of divine necessity, but
rather of invitation. She claims that taking up one's cross every day is a
metaphor for mission, not suffering. By definition, the cross is a once-
in-a-lifetime event and therefore cannot be taken up every day. Instead,
"the assumption of God's mission demands the kind of ultimate loyalty
that allows one to set aside one's fear of death. It therefore involves the
willingness to pursue the mission even at one's peril. But the mission is
not defined by suffering."[143]

Schertz finds that there are two places in Luke's gospel where he
uses the language of divine necessity regarding suffering for the disciples
(Luke 12:11–12; 18:1). However, the narrative context of those passages
is a discussion of trust, not suffering. The disciples must necessarily
trust in God when they are brought before the authorities, for as Schertz
observes:

> Certainly Luke recognizes that taking up the mission of God
> will sometimes put disciples into perilous situations. But what is
> necessary for disciples is not to suffer but to trust in God in dan-
> gerous situations which might entail suffering. Again, the em-
> phasis is on mission. Suffering is understood as an occupational
> hazard of the mission but it does not define the mission.[144]

Although suffering does not define the mission and should not be
valorized, it should not be avoided at all costs. Schertz explains, "If someone is suffering because she is actively engaged in God's mission, because
she is proclaiming and enacting the kingdom of God, then from a bibli-
cal-theology perspective such suffering must be defended and supported
as redemptive."[145] Because Schertz claims that proclaiming and enacting
the kingdom is salvific, the sacrificial suffering that often comes with
those actions also has a part in redemption. In this way, Schertz claims

142. Ibid., 203, 206.
143. Ibid., 204.
144. Ibid.
145. Ibid., 207.

that her model provides a corrective to the types of feminist theology that have no space for sacrifice.[146] However, she is also quick to point out that the suffering Christians may have to endure as they are proclaiming and enacting the kingdom is not victimization.[147] It is not passive suffering. Instead, it is the result of active confrontation with the status quo.

In some ways, Schertz's model offers a corrective to some of the problems noted in other models in this chapter. Schertz highlights all of the key Anabaptist emphases that the others do, but she takes feminist critiques of suffering seriously by distinguishing different kinds of suffering. In this way, it seems Schertz offers a corrective for feminist theories that allow absolutely no place for any kind of suffering for any reason.

Summary

Each of the models we have analyzed in this chapter seems to delay salvation—or at least earthly salvation—to some point in the future. For example, Schertz calls this ultimate salvation the kingdom of God, and there is much biblical and traditional precedent for such a move. From very early on in the Jesus movement, Christians have talked about the already and not-yet qualities of salvation. That is, Jesus and his atoning actions offer some sort of salvation, but complete salvation will not come until the eschaton. Surely that was a hopeful thought for the first generation of Christians who were waiting for Jesus' return. But after two thousand years of waiting, when life has improved, yet continues to be held and influenced by the powers and principalities, perhaps we need to change our understanding of the not-yet quality of salvation. Schertz writes that we are to trust in God, but for what exactly do we trust God? It seems that when we are confronted by such difficult questions, we tend to lapse into traditional religious language that, although it may seem to solve the problem, is not especially meaningful in our postmodern

146. Ibid.

147. Ibid. In his discussion of the similarities of the early Brethren and Søren Kierkegaard, Vernard Eller claims that Kierkegaard "was particularly incensed against the sort of preaching that is quick to credit the patient endurance of every affliction and inconvenience as being *Christian* suffering" (Eller, *Kierkegaard and Radical Discipleship*, 397, emphasis in original). In this way, Eller echoes Schertz's argument that suffering itself should not be valorized or considered redemptive. Instead, it should only be endured and supported as a result of the active proclamation and enactment of the kingdom of God in confrontation with the world.

worldview. In order for a Brethren theory of atonement to be relevant to contemporary believers, it must not fall into this language trap.

Many of the models we have analyzed so far offer compelling and at-tractive components for a Brethren view of atonement. Not surprisingly, these components often reflect historical Anabaptist and Pietist empha-ses. First, these models place special emphasis on the life and teachings of Jesus because together they form the pattern of discipleship that Chris-tians are to follow. Early Anabaptists took Jesus' teachings seriously, and they strove to live lives and create a community based on those teachings. Contemporary Anabaptist theologians pick up this emphasis and apply it to salvation. Not only are Christians supposed to follow literally Jesus' teachings, but correctly following those teachings is also crucial to salva-tion. According to both Anabaptist and Pietist theology, there can be no split between faith and life. For Anabaptist soteriology, there can be no split between salvation and ethics or a life of discipleship. James McClen-don writes, "The strength of this plan of salvation lay in the tight bond it created between divine grace and a total human response. Christian conduct did not follow (by some kind of inference or induction) as a consequence of salvation: it *was itself* salvation. The salvific gift of God and its human answer in following Jesus were two sides of one reality."[148] In other words, the life of discipleship is God's gift of salvation.

These models also stress that the way of God is different from the way of the world. That Jesus is the clearest revelation of God (and God's will for humanity) means Jesus' nonviolent way of life reveals God's will: that humans act nonviolently toward one another. Jesus reveals through his confrontation with the power structures of the world that the king-dom of God has a different set of priorities. Relationships in the kingdom of God are not characterized by retributive justice or violent punishment, but instead by reconciliation and healing. In this way, salvation, for many Anabaptists, begins in the here and now. Just as they reject models of atonement that place all of the drama outside of human history and thus deny the importance of a human response, so too do many Anabaptist theologians bring salvation back from the cosmic realm so that it has an earthly component. For example, Gordon Kaufman writes that salvation is "that special quality [that] human life is expected to take on within this new community, with its straining toward truly humane patterns of ex-istence within itself and its larger task of fostering further humanization

---

148. McClendon, *Doctrine*, 118, emphasis in original.

in the world through a ministry of healing and reconciliation."[149] That is, salvation produces some kind of effect in this world.

Finally, many of these models stress Jesus' resurrection as proof that the way of Jesus is the way of God. They see in the gospel witness that the way of Jesus is not the way of the world, and they interpret the resurrection as God's validation of Jesus' way. McClendon articulates this view by writing, "The resurrection was God's sign of self-identification with Jesus, who had taken the nonviolent way of the cross. It was God's way, God's *only* way . . . The chief obstacle of [the disciples'] faith, the cross, became the chief content of their faith. God's rule, by way of the cross, prevailed."[150] The resurrection affirms that Jesus is indeed Lord and is ultimately in charge of history. This affirmation gives Christians the courage they need to follow in Jesus' way—to life a life of discipleship modeled on his life and ministry—even though it means that they will necessarily confront the ways and powers of the world and likely endure suffering.

Drawing on the positive elements of these models, perhaps we can construct a list of the qualities or points that a good Brethren model of atonement must have. Such a model must contain the following:

- An emphasis on Jesus' life, ministry, and teaching

- Acknowledgement that the way of God and Jesus is different from the ways of the world

- Appreciation of the fact that God does not will the suffering or death of Jesus—or of anyone

- An awareness that Jesus' death was caused by humans who opposed his way of living (i.e., was not willed by God)

- A role for the follower that entails a life of some kind of discipleship

- Recognition that God and Jesus are nonviolent, which means that we must be as well

- A communal or social element so that salvation is not just a matter for individuals

- A real and transformative effect on the world and not just an emotional or psychological effect on believers

---

149. Kaufman, *In Face of Mystery*, 407.

150. McClendon, *Doctrine*, 236, emphasis in original.

- An effect on the earth here and now that does not rely on action that takes place outside of human history or a reward that is received only after death

- An allowance for the imagination and creativity of God to act in unexpected ways

All of these elements were noted in one form or another in at least one of the models presented in this chapter. But there are other elements necessary for an adequate model:

- A meaningful engagement with a postmodern worldview

  » Such engagement includes being clear and honest in the model's language and not falling back into traditional religious language without defining what those terms mean in contemporary terms. This includes mention of the resurrection. An adequate model must make sense of the resurrection in a way that is consistent with the postmodern view of miracles.

  » This postmodern worldview must include the insights of science. There are too many Christians who operate in a kind of schizophrenic fashion insofar as they see the world in one way for six days out of the week, but on Sunday, they go to church and believe something completely different. An adequate model cannot allow this.

  » This model cannot be exclusivist. Postmodernity has stripped away the notion of a single grand narrative that folds all the details of history into a single trajectory that conforms to some ultimate plan for the world.[151] Therefore, an adequate model for contemporary believers who are aware of the diversity of people and faiths in the world cannot affirm that Jesus is the only way to God or the only path to salvation. Taking the astronomical discoveries of the past few centuries into account, Sallie McFague acknowledges that the exclusivism of much traditional theology is preposterous:

    > The scandal of uniqueness is absolutized by Christianity into one of its central doctrines, which claims that God is embodied in one place and one place only: in the man Jesus of Nazareth. He and he alone is "the image of the invisible God" (Col. 1:15). The source, power, and goal of the universe is known through

151. See Kraybill and Eisenbise, *Brethren in Postmodern World*, 6–9.

and only through a first-century Mediterranean carpenter. The creator and redeemer of the fifteen-billion-year history of the universe with its hundred billion galaxies (and their billions of stars and planets) is available only in a thirty-year span of one human being's life on planet earth. The claim, when put in the context of contemporary science, seems skewed, to say the least. When the world consisted of the Roman Empire (with "barbarians" at its frontiers), the limitation of divine presence to Jesus of Nazareth had some plausibility while still being ethnocentric; but for many hundreds of years, well before contemporary cosmology, the claims of other major religious traditions have seriously challenged it. In its traditional form the claim is not only offensive to the integrity and value of other religions, but incredible, indeed, absurd, in light of postmodern cosmology. It is not remotely compatible with our current picture of the universe.[152]

Therefore, a postmodern Brethren theory of atonement must find a balance between highlighting the importance of Jesus' life and ministry for our own ethical actions and acknowledging that all of God's creativity, imagination, love, and power cannot possibly be contained in this one human person who is completely insignificant on the scale of cosmic history.

- A willingness to let go some of the elements of traditional theology that no longer make sense with the way we understand ourselves and the world

In other words, an adequate model of atonement for contemporary Brethren believers must hold the unique theological beliefs of the early Anabaptists and Radical Pietists together with the most important features of postmodern thought. In the following chapter, we shall attempt to construct just such a model.

---

152. McFague, *Body of God*, 159.

CHAPTER 5

Cooperative Salvation: A Constructive Brethren Model of Atonement

As noted earlier, the past few decades have seen a renewed interest in atonement theory. Theologians from many different backgrounds have proposed noteworthy models, but few of these models have the distinctive elements of Brethren theology. And most of the Brethren theology written recently has looked backwards, having been more interested in Brethren history than constructive theology. Therefore, the task of this chapter is to propose a forward-looking model of atonement that takes up distinctive Anabaptist and Pietist ideas and uses them in a way that makes sense in a contemporary Brethren worldview. We will try to incorporate all of the characteristics listed at the end of the previous chapter into a logical and meaningful model of atonement.

However, we must be clear that parts of this model diverge from the understandings of the earliest Anabaptists, Pietists, and Brethren. While this divergence may seem problematic to some, it is nonetheless necessary, given that contemporary Brethren believers operate out of a different framework than did our earliest spiritual ancestors. Contemporary believers tend to have a wider view of the world, a greater facility with science, and more exposure to people of different faiths. Thus, the proposed model will incorporate elements of traditional Brethren theology, but will weave them together with ideas that are important to contemporary believers.

Any model of atonement must answer four basic questions. First, what is the problem? What is wrong with humanity and our relationship with God that necessitates atonement of some sort? Second, what is Jesus' role in atonement? How do his life, death, and resurrection solve the problem? Third, what is God's role in all of this? Finally, what is the effect of atonement? Here we are asking about salvation. What does the salvation that Jesus brings look like? The following sections address each of these questions in turn.

The Problem

All of the world's religions start with the assumption that there is something wrong—with us or with the world. Things are not as they should be. How religions diagnose that problem and propose to fix it varies quite a bit, but they all start at this point.[1] Obviously, how they diagnose the problem leads to very different solutions. Traditional Christian theology has diagnosed the problem as sin. The solution to that problem is atonement, and the goal of Christianity has been salvation. But, as we have noted in the previous two chapters, many contemporary theologians argue that the concept of sin must be expanded if it is to contain the whole of the human problem. A contemporary Brethren view should follow their lead.

Most people today would agree that the world is not as it should be. It is rife with suffering of all kinds, including the deterioration and exploitation of the natural world. But what is the cause of that suffering? Traditional theology teaches us that the cause is disobedience and desire. Usually this explanation relies on the story of Adam and Eve. Because these first humans desired the fruit they could not have and disobeyed God's only rule, all subsequent humans are fallen away from their original state of being, which was created in the image of God. We are damaged and depraved to the point that sin and sinfulness make up the core of our being.[2] While it is true that there are depraved people in the world, to say that depravity is our deepest and primary human characteristic does not ring true with my own experience or with Anabaptist theological anthropology.

From the beginning of the movement, Anabaptists did not begin their theology with the crushing awareness of being sinners. In fact, they rejected the idea of original sin because it meant that Christ's

---

1. See Prothero, *God Is Not One*, 11.

2. For an example of this traditional theology, see Sproul, *Essential Truths*, 147–49.

righteousness would have to save all people at once, instead of only those who had been transformed by his righteousness and lived in discipleship. They argued that all people are not automatically infected with Adam's sin; in order to be sinful, people had to act sinfully. They viewed sin as a conscious choice rather than as an inborn disease beyond one's control.[3] Early Anabaptists quoted Ezek 18:20 to support their rejection of inherited sin.[4] In fact, this idea is one reason why the Anabaptists insisted on adult believers' baptism. They did not worry about the eternal damnation of their children's souls before the age of baptism because they did not believe in inherited sin.[5] In other words, people are not born into sin, but live into it. Sin is defined in their actions, not their existence. The early Anabaptists rejected the notion of bondage of the will or predestination because if humanity were as sinful and depraved as mainstream Protestant anthropology suggests, discipleship would be futile.[6] They reasoned that God would not command us to obey if we did not have the ability to obey the divine commandments.[7]

3. Friedmann, *Theology of Anabaptism*, 62–63.

4. "The person who sins shall die. A child shall not suffer for the iniquity of a parent, nor a parent suffer for the iniquity of a child; the righteousness of the righteous shall be his own, and the wickedness of the wicked shall be his own."

5. Mack, "Basic Questions," 30–31.

6. Snyder, *Anabaptist History and Theology*, 86. Early Anabaptists also rejected the idea of original sin. Thomas Friedmann quotes Sebastian Franck's *Chronica, Zeytbuch und Geschychtsbibel* from 1531 to show that Anabaptists rejected the idea of original sin because it meant that Christ's righteousness would have to save all people at once, instead of only those who had been transformed by his righteousness and lived in discipleship: "Concerning original sin nearly all Anabaptists teach as follows: Just as the righteousness of Christ is of no avail unless he makes it part of his own through faith, so also Adam's sin does not impair anybody except the one who makes it a part of his own being and brings forth the fruits of his sin. For as foreign righteousness does not save anybody, so will foreign sin not condemn anybody either" (Friedmann, *Theology of Anabaptism*, 62–63).

7. Balthasar Hubmaier explained humanity's ability to follow God's commandments through a tripartite anthropology separated into the spirit, soul, and body. The body is worthless, but the spirit is happy and willing and ready for all good, while the soul stands in between the two. In this way, Hubmaier blames the soul for its corruption but exonerates the spirit from all blemish. The spirit remains upright and intact before, during, and after the fall. Thus, the spirit allows us to connect to divine grace and divine commandments and become restored to the full image of God. No total depravity is ever possible, because the human core remains uncorrupted and able to grasp God's grace and goodness. Something in humanity has remained good and unspoiled, which makes us fully responsible for our actions (Friedmann, *Theology of Anabaptism*, 58–60).

Clearly, early Anabaptists had a more positive theological anthropology than did the mainline Reformers, but they still understood sin
to be a problem and primarily saw it as disobedience, especially an
unwillingness to follow Jesus' example. But does this understanding of
sin as disobedience and desire continue to make sense in a postmodern
worldview that understands humanity in an evolutionary context? Is all
the conflict in and between ourselves and in the world because of sin?
According to evolutionary science, the desire for material goods and the
conflict that results from those desires are a product of the way we have
evolved. To not desire and attain those goods would be suicidal—we need
them to live.[8] Self-concern is natural and even necessary for survival; we
are hardwired to attend to our own needs first. Although we are capable
of experiencing feelings of altruism and empathy during times of peace
and safety, our primary concern reverts to self-preservation during times
of stress. Wendy Farley notes this in her atonement model. She writes, "It
is natural and appropriate that our awareness of our own embodied self
is much more vivid than our awareness of other things. The vividness is
a good thing: hunger makes us feed ourselves; pain makes us remove our
hand from the fire. When these responses are damaged . . . one's very life
can be at risk."[9] Farley does not think that this process of self-preservation
is an evil phenomenon; this is just the way that human evolution works.
In this way, these desires themselves must be good. The problem arises,
however, when our desires become all-consuming, especially when the
drive to fulfill them blots out awareness and concern for others. When we
slide permanently into the belief that our own pains and difficulties are
more important than the needs of others, or even that ours are the only
desires or problems that exist, this is sin. The problem is living in a permanent state of self-focus. Farley labels this phenomenon egocentrism,
and I would extend this idea to say that it is a kind of self-absorption. We
are often so absorbed by our own problems and concerns that we cannot
even see the problems of others. Farley rightly notes, "My intellectual
knowledge that I am not one iota more important or real than anyone
or anything else does not translate into felt experience . . . Egocentrism
is like the dentist's drill that has slipped past the reach of Novocain.
When that happens, our pain is all we can experience."[10] Attention to our

8. See Williams, *Doing without Adam and Eve*, 148.

9. Ibid., 33.

10. Farley, *Wounding and Healing*, 49, 50.

own pain is not sinful; it is natural and necessary. But awareness of our own sufferings and desires cannot become all-consuming. When we are oblivious to the concerns of others, we become alienated from them, and this is the root of the human problem. This isolation is the hell that John Howard Yoder aptly described in his atonement model.[11] Perhaps, then, alienation from others because of self-absorption and extreme selfishness is a better way for contemporary believers to understand sin.

Again, it is important to note that our human desires or self-concern is not the problem, though theologians dating all the way back to Augustine have argued such. They claimed that pride and a desire for power over others are at the root of all human sinfulness and that the way to overcome sin is through humility and self-negation.[12] There are two glaring problems with this conception of sin. First, we have been conditioned through evolution to desire power over others or to be associated with those who have power over others. That is one of the ways we assure our own survival and the survival of our group. Therefore, this desire cannot simply be dismissed as the fundamental problem with humanity. The second problem is revealed by feminist theologian Judith Plaskow when she notes that a desire for power over others is often a "male perspective" of sin, explaining that society encourages men to seek power over others while women are socialized to put themselves second and submit to men's power.[13] Cynthia Crysdale picks up this critique in her own atonement model, noting that counseling a victim to repent of his or her pride ends up blaming the victim for his or her own suffering.[14] Clearly, this definition of sin is not appropriate for those on the underside of power relations in society.

However, if we think of sin as any action or inclination that prevents us from being in right and full relationship with others—and therefore with God—then our definition is flexible and personal enough that it accommodates Plaskow's and Crysdale's critiques. If women follow society's norms by always putting themselves second and submitting their own desires to the will of others, they cannot be in full and right relationship with others because they have not brought their full selves to the

---

11. See ibid., 86–87; and Yoder, *Preface to Theology*, 280.

12. This linking of pride and evil as well as humility and redemption is an important theme throughout the entirety of Augustine's *Confessions*.

13. See Plaskow, *Sex, Sin, and Grace*, especially 165–69.

14. Crysdale, *Embracing Travail*, 25.

relationship.[15] Conversely, if men follow society's norms by always asserting themselves over others, they too cannot be in full and right relationship. The postmodern worldview appreciates difference and refuses to
pretend that there are universal experiences or objective categories into
which every person can fit. Therefore, we need a more elastic and subjective definition of sin because the action that alienates another in one
situation might be the same action that draws someone into relationship
in another situation.

The problem of sin is not just about individual actions, however.
Liberation and feminist theologians have persuasively argued that sin is
larger than any individual or his or her actions. Those who have power
want to keep it, so they build societal structures that serve to ensure the
survival and protection of their own interests, their own power, and their
own status within the social hierarchy. Once these systems are in place,
they become larger than any person or group of individuals, as Walter
Wink has rightly noted. They become forces that are woven into the
structure and relationships of society. We become bound to these forces,
which together comprise the domination system. We did not necessarily
create the elements of this system, but we all continue to live in and under
them. Gustavo Gutiérrez calls this the "collective dimensions of sin," and
argues that it is "evident in oppressive structures, in the exploitation of
humans by humans, in the domination and slavery of peoples, races, and
social classes."[16]

Rosemary Radford Ruether offers a compelling example of this kind
of collective dimension of sin in her construction of sexism as original
sin.[17] She argues that the fall is the systemic alienation from God that
results in the distortion of gender into unjust structures of domination
and subordination. Sexism and the distorted relationships that result
from it are examples of the powers and principalities of historic, systemic, and social evil that condition our choices from before our birth.
In other words, these distorted relationships are the cultural baggage
that we inherit. In this way, we all bear the consequences of this sin even

---

15. Wendy Farley echoes this sentiment: "Sin is not only the distortion of arro-
gance and strengths [traditional views of sin] but also the weakness whereby those
who are downtrodden or lacking in confidence or who allow themselves, wittingly
and unwittingly, to be exploited by oppressive forces bind themselves to small and
distorted expressions of their beauty and power" (Farley, *Wounding and Healing*, 24).

16. Gutiérrez, *Theology of Liberation*, 103.

17. Ruether, *Sexism and God-Talk*, 173–83.

though we are not individually responsible for its inception. The sin of distorted gender relationships is obviously not just an individual reality and therefore demands the conversion of all, not just as individuals but as a collective system. Surely, this view of original sin as the systems we are born into and benefit from (though not because of our own choosing or our own actions) makes much more sense to contemporary believers than original sin as a genetic flaw.

When we put all of these ideas together, we can say that the chief problem with humanity is that we are isolated and alienated from one another, not just by our individual actions, but also by the systems and structures that order our lives.[18] It appears that we have evolved to have competing desires—not only for material goods and personal power, but also for community. The best way to solve the human problem of isolation and alienation is to find a way to balance those competing desires. We can say, then, that atonement is the process by which we achieve that balance so that we do right by ourselves, but also care for the other— whether that is other people, the environment, or God.

Jesus' Role

The way we achieve that balance might be as individualized as our concept of sin. Christianity has argued that the best way to know how to live in right relationship with God and with others is to look to the example of Jesus, and indeed, Jesus provides helpful clues about how to find that balance. A brief glance through the gospels reveals that Jesus was concerned about humanity on three levels: caring for the self, caring for individuals and maintaining individual relationships, and caring about social relationships and the ways that domination systems affect individuals and societies. Often, these concerns intertwined and overlapped.

In terms of caring for the self, Jesus did not advocate that his followers give up all of their own needs or desires to follow him and be a part of his ministry. His disciples did not have to abandon all of their earthly desires. The criticisms lodged against Jesus, namely that he dined with drunkards and gluttons (Matt 11:18–19; Luke 7:33–35), imply that he and his disciples certainly honored some of their material wants. Also,

---

18. It is important to note that these powers are not all bad, nor do they always serve to alienate us from one another. Wink provides a helpfully nuanced description of the good and evil qualities of the powers. See Wink, *Engaging the Powers*, 65–73.

Jesus did not counsel his followers to be submissive, to endure suffering purely for the sake of suffering itself, or to give up their dignity in order to avoid confrontation with one another.[19] Walter Wink's descriptions of Jesus' third way (exemplified by turning the other cheek, stripping naked, and going the second mile) proves that Jesus taught his followers that they should preserve their dignity, and thus, care for their own selves. Wendy Farley also notes that self-sacrifice can and should be viewed as a form of violence, especially when "it disguises the dissipation of our personhood."[20] Although later Christian tradition has emphasized the virtuousness of suffering and counseled Christians to suffer like Jesus, that advice seems contrary to Jesus' own actions and teachings. In this way, the Anabaptist insistence on basing its theology more on the example of Jesus than on the traditions of the church answers the feminist critique of Christian valorization of suffering.

But Jesus did not advocate concern for the self alone. He also viewed maintaining relationships with other individuals as an important part of his ministry. Often, these relationships served to undermine the domination systems that held people in their grasp, such as in the case of the woman at the well (John 4:1–26), but he also seems to have genuinely cared for those around him. We see this in his care and concern for Mary and Martha, the beloved disciple, and Peter.[21]

These concerns for the self and for individuals are present in the gospel accounts of Jesus' ministry, but they are far outweighed by the number of times Jesus confronts the systems of oppression under which the people suffered. Perhaps this is because the drive to care for ourselves and those closest to or most like us is natural. We do not need much encouragement to protect those instinctive interests, but to resist the powers is both physically and socially unnatural in that doing so is often not in our immediate best interests. Therefore, it makes sense that most of Jesus' ministry would be devoted to this teaching.

The gospel accounts of Jesus' life and ministry highlight several concerns that point to Jesus' denunciation of the domination system: a concern for those at the margins of society; a concern for justice, particularly

19. Despite what many Brethren may think, confrontation and conflict are not sinful and do not prevent good relationships.

20. Farley, *Wounding and Healing*, 84.

21. For example, see Luke 10:38–42 and John 11:32–33 on Jesus' love for Mary and Martha; John 13:23–25, 19:26–27, 20:1–10, 21:21–25, 21:24 regarding the beloved disciple, and Matt 16:17–19 concerning Peter.

economic justice; upending hierarchies and the status quo; commitment to nonviolent action; and refusing to use power over others. Jesus consistently critiqued the dominant systems of power and their power holders and denounced their exploitative practices. He rejected the practices of those in power and himself refused to use power over others. Walter Wink aptly describes the ways Jesus undermined the domination system:

> In his Beatitudes, in his extraordinary concern for the outcasts and marginalized, in his wholly unconventional treatment of women, in his love for children, and in his rejection of the belief that high-ranking men are the favorites of God, in his subversive proclamation of a new order in which domination will give way to compassion and communion . . . almost every sentence Jesus uttered [and almost every action he performed] was an indictment of the domination system or the disclosure of an alternative to it.[22]

Jesus showed great concern for the other, especially others who were oppressed by these systems. He certainly did not allow his own naturally evolved human desires to dictate all of his actions, and thus he overcame the human problem and was sinless. In this model, Jesus faces all the same natural temptations to slip into a permanent state of self-focus that the rest of us do. In fact, Jesus' temptation by the devil in the wilderness metaphorically depicts his natural human temptation. First, he is tempted to live by bread alone, meaning to care only for his physical desires (Luke 4:2b–4). Second, he is tempted to give in to the domination systems (Luke 4:5–8). Third, he is tempted to gain glory and status for himself, perhaps to lord it over others (Luke 4:9–12). The temptation stories illustrate the inauguration of Jesus' ministry of alternative options. Although the gospel narratives employ mythical language to tell this story, we can easily imagine that these stories point to Jesus' very human temptations to claim power for himself and to use it for his own benefit or glory. Yet, he overcomes these temptations, and that is how he offers salvation. What makes him a savior, then, is not his preexistence or his distinctive metaphysical nature. Jesus was human like all the rest of us are human. But he was special in that he was able to maintain the balance between self and others, and he offers salvation in that he models the pattern for us.[23]

22. Wink, *Powers That Be*, 63–64. See also ibid., *Engaging the Powers*, 111–37.

23. The Christology I am proposing here certainly breaks with traditional Brethren views of Jesus. And while the cooperative salvation model of atonement may not

Clearly, this atonement model is subjective. Jesus does not do anything for us outside the boundaries of human history. Jesus and God do not work out some special arrangement that changes our fallen human nature. Fallenness does not make sense in a postmodern worldview informed by science. But isolation and alienation do. Therefore, this model offers a way for us to overcome our individual and social alienation by following Jesus' lived example. If we follow his model, we too will be healed of our alienation; we will be saved. Jesus does not offer atonement on our behalf; he provides a model that we might follow in order to atone ourselves.

Salvation, in this model, depends on Jesus' life and ministry. It has nothing to do with his death. His suffering and death on the cross are not salvific, and they do *not* reveal God's love for us. Instead, this gruesome act is one more (if possibly the ultimate) example of the true, repulsive nature of the domination system. It was individuals in power, and especially the structures of a domination system that benefitted the powerful, that murdered Jesus. Many of the authors in the previous two chapters have come to this conclusion as well. Denny Weaver writes that the "powers of evil need [Jesus'] death in order to remove his challenge to their power."[24] Similarly, Walter Wink believes that the powers had to kill Jesus because he "represented the most intolerable threat ever placed against the spirituality, values, and arrangements of the Domination System."[25] The perpetrators of demonic power (those who used power to exploit others) recognized in Jesus' actions a different way of living that sought to dismantle the oppressive structures keeping them in power. Jesus' death was deplorable, just as all deaths that result from the workings of the domination system are deplorable. Nothing good happened on Good Friday; Jesus' death was neither salvific nor willed by God. God's will for the world as modeled in Jesus' life is one in which all life is treated with dignity, not a world in which one person can be exploited and tortured for the benefit of others. Jesus' suffering and death were tragic rather than salvific. And the continued suffering and deaths

---

require such a low Christology, this view of Jesus reemphasizes the point that we are responsible for our own salvation. We can't fall back on a divine savior to do the work for us. Additionally, we can't ignore the fact that there are people of other faiths working for cooperative salvation. Positing a human Jesus allows for collaboration between many different groups of people, which is one of the signs of salvation.

24. Weaver, *Nonviolent Atonement*, 72.

25. Wink, *Engaging the Powers*, 110.

at the hands of the domination system is just as tragic. This model follows others we have examined in declaring that nothing good came of Jesus' death. It was not willed by God.

Jesus' suffering and death were not salvific, but the actions that led to that suffering were and are salvific. His actions, which threatened the domination system in order to lift up the least of these, offer the model we are to follow in order to experience salvation. If we work similarly to resist the domination system, we will enter into right relationship with God and those for whom God cares. But we will also put ourselves at risk, just like Jesus did. Those who resist the system most often suffer at the hands of the system. That does not make such suffering good in any way. The feminist critics are correct when they argue that there is nothing good about suffering. Suffering simply for the sake of suffering is not godly; it is pointless and harmful. However, those critics go too far when they imply that suffering should be avoided at all costs because it is detrimental to the self. For example, Rebecca Parker and Rita Nakashima Brock argue that Martin Luther King Jr.'s nonviolent actions during the civil rights movement should not be emulated simply because he took on suffering himself in order to change the hearts and minds of those who killed him. They argue that this model requires everything of the victim and nothing of the perpetrators, which further counsels Christians to accept their own suffering.[26] Of course the self must be protected, as Jesus' own actions showed. But when our own protection becomes our only concern, we slip back into sin. Suffering alone—whether Jesus' or our own—is not salvific. But working against the domination system in order to improve the lives of others does lead to salvation. Working on behalf of others puts us in right relationship with those others, even as we suffer with them. Once again, the key to this model is finding the correct balance between concern for self and concern for others.

God's Role

As we saw at the very beginning of this book, the question of why Jesus died has been a difficult one throughout all of Christian history. Scores of different atonement models have been proposed to try to make sense of this fact, and as we have seen, some are more successful than others. Some require extreme mental gymnastics to try to make sense of

---

26. Brock and Parker, *Proverbs of Ashes*, 40–42.

why God would allow such a horrific event to occur. Even those models that affirm that God did not will Jesus' death or that Jesus' death is not salvific do not offer a convincing explanation as to why God allowed it to happen. This shortcoming is the principal drawback of Abelard's moral influence theory and of many contemporary theories that fall into the same category.

If God has the power to make everything right and to save Jesus from a torturous death but simply chose not to do it, then this is a very cruel God. Process theologian Robert Mesle says it best in describing why much of traditional theology's view of God is unacceptable: "At the very best, God has been depicted as standing by and allowing needless suffering that 'He' could have easily prevented. To defend our ideas of God, we are driven to turn our ideas of good and evil inside out to explain why it is really good for God to allow such great suffering."[27] Mesle has in mind the generalized suffering experienced by so many in this world, but his critique takes on special meaning when we apply it to generations of atonement theory. As we have seen, theologians have proposed all sorts of models in an effort to simultaneously hold together the ideas that God is all powerful and all loving, and yet that Jesus died an excruciating, humiliating death. So many of these models are unsatisfying because they require the innocent suffering of Jesus. Even those models that do not make Jesus' suffering and death the center of how God effects atonement still require his death in one way or another. Otherwise, God is a horrible monster who allows Jesus to suffer and die for no reason.

The reason the Christian tradition has clung to the notion of an omnipotent God is rooted in our desire for power. We visualize God as an omnipotent lord because ultimate power is our own ultimate goal: "A deity who most instantiates what much of society most admires . . . would precisely be a powerful, invulnerable God . . . This is the sort of God to whom speakers at political conventions appeal or pray to bless America."[28] If we cannot have ultimate power ourselves, then at least we can worship a God who does. We can rest in the knowledge that although we are weak and powerless now (just like Jesus was), eventually we will be on God's winning side when all things come to an end. Eventually, God will use God's own power for our benefit. Although John Howard Yoder is adamant in his claim that Christian disciples should not desire power

27. Mesle, *Process Theology*, 5.

28. Placher, *Narratives of a Vulnerable God*, 6.

and should not be concerned with exerting power in the world, his whole theology seems to rest on the hope that God's power will eventually rectify all the damage done and vindicate all those who appeared weak in the eyes of the world. He argues that nonresistance is right, not because it is effective, but because it anticipates the triumph of the slain Lamb.[29] Yoder writes, "Jesus did not free His disciples from violence to make them pure and weak, but because He called them to use other, stronger resources."[30] Even if those resources are nonviolent and loving, Yoder's model still appeals to God's power.

But this is not God's way, as we see in Jesus' ministry. One of the key convictions of Anabaptist theology has always been that Jesus provides the best glimpse humans can get of God and God's ways. Again and again, Jesus refused to grasp power for his own benefit or for the benefit of others. Walter Wink and John Howard Yoder both argue convincingly that this is the whole point of the gospels' depictions of Jesus' wilderness temptations. Jesus broke with the continuities of human civilizations and the loyalties of human societies, and his actions must reflect God's denunciation of such uses of power. Therefore, it seems odd and inconsistent that many contemporary Anabaptist theologians who recognize Jesus' refusal to grasp power continue to employ some kind of modified *Christus Victor* theory. After all, this model rests on God's powerful actions in vindicating Jesus in the resurrection and eventually completely ridding the world of evil. This model seems to contrast Jesus' actions and God's actions rather than appearing to highlight the continuity of will between Jesus and God. Furthermore, even in its contemporary reinterpretations, this model still does not answer the question of why God is waiting to bring about that complete victory. If God has the power to do so, what is God waiting for?

The most satisfying answer to this question comes from process theology, which answers simply that God does not have the power to do so. God doesn't end all suffering because God can't end all suffering.

According to process theology, God is not omnipotent in the traditional sense. God does not affect the world through coercive power by making things happen according to God's will. Rather than being a removed, impassible, almighty being who affects the world but is not affected by it, God is in intimate relationship with the world, suffering

---

29. Yoder, *Royal Priesthood*, 151.

30. Ibid., "Jesus and Power," 371.

when we suffer and elated when we are joyous. God cares deeply for the world and wants what is best for us, for the planet, and indeed for all of the cosmos. But God is not in control of the universe the way traditional theology has imagined it, as one who makes events happen. Instead, God's power is persuasive. God cares for and interacts with the universe by luring all of creation to the best possible outcome or its self-actualization. That is, "God's work in the world should be understood as that of persuading every entity to attain some optimum of satisfaction compatible with the maintenance of an order which enables others also to attain their satisfaction."[31]

God's action is much more subtle, if perhaps less effective than has traditionally been imagined in that all aspects of the cosmos retain the ability to reject God and God's luring: "God seeks to persuade each occasion toward the possibility for its own existence which would be best for it, given its context; but God cannot control the finite occasion's self-actualization. Accordingly, the divine creative activity involves risk."[32] Responding to this divine creative activity involves risk as well, and not just the risk that we will encounter suffering (like Jesus did when he confronted the powers), but the risk that that suffering will not be vindicated. While suffering at the hands of the powerful is never easy, perhaps it becomes easier when one is able to rest in the knowledge that one's suffering will be vindicated when God decides to step in and set things right. But following Jesus' model of renouncing power over others becomes much more difficult without the assurance of a powerful and almighty God.[33] Wendy Farley notes, "In the midst of our suffering, imagining that God really does not control events can seem more terrifying than imagining that God uses violence, war, injustice, and disease 'for our own good.'"[34] Or, in Robert Mesle's words, "The battle between good and evil is a real one. God cannot guarantee the outcome within this world."[35] God can-

---

31. Cobb, *God and the World*, 94.

32. Cobb and Griffin, *Process Theology*, 53.

33. Indeed, this difficulty is precisely what Jürgen Moltmann believes is the correct interpretation of Christianity. He writes, "Thus at the level of the psychology of religion, Christian faith effects liberation from the childish projections of human needs for the riches of God; liberation from human impotence for the omnipotence of God; from human helplessness for the responsibility of God" (Moltmann, *Crucified God*, 216).

34. Farley, *Wounding and Healing*, 96.

35. Mesle, *Process Theology*, 16.

not guarantee the outcome of the universe or time either. Under process theology, the future is an open risk. God's persuasive power for good is effective only insofar as creatures affirm that good.[36] In this way, the future is unknown, even to God, for all of creation retains the absolute freedom to accept or reject God's invitation to goodness. If we affirm this notion of God, the fundamental affirmation of the *Christus Victor* theory falls away—and with it all the problems of viewing Christ as a king and triumphant lord.

While the idea that God is not in complete control of the universe may be terrifying and perhaps even un-Christian to some, the idea that God wishes to stop the world's suffering but cannot is surely more reassuring than the idea that God can stop that suffering but for some reason chooses not to do so. It seems to me that a loving God who wishes to stop suffering is more worthy of worship than a God who withholds that power for some unknown reason. Therefore, we must reject the *Christus Victor* model of atonement and any other model that relies on the power of God to triumph over the power of evil. Otherwise, we get caught up in the notion of a superhuman God. A process notion of God seems much more in line with human experience as well as with a scientific understanding of the world that rejects an interventionist God, and it also fits nicely into this model of atonement.

If we accept the idea that God is not in complete control of the universe, we are provided an easy answer to why God allowed Jesus to be murdered: God could not stop it. Perhaps Jesus came to this realization himself as he asked, "My God, my God, why have you forsaken me?" (Mark 15:34; Matt 27:46; Ps 22:1). Perhaps we witness in this agonizing question Jesus' own dawning realization that God is not in control of the world.

If we accept that God's power is persuasive rather than coercive, then only a subjective theory of atonement makes sense. Jesus' life and ministry presents us with God's invitation to live in a way that is caring and compassionate for ourselves and for others, and it is up to each individual to accept or reject that invitation. The result of our actions—our atonement—does not change the nature of God or change God's mind about us (as it would under an objective theory). But God does participate in our experience of our chosen actions. When we choose to act in a way that maximizes our relationships and minimizes our isolation, God

36. Ford, "Divine Persuasion," 140.

rejoices in our salvation. When we choose to maximize our own power over others, God suffers with us in the depths of our hell and isolation.

In this model, salvation rests on our choosing to follow the example of Jesus' life. It has nothing to do with his death, and in that way, it makes a huge break from most Christian theology. But given the pain that has been done in the name of traditional theology (such as the woman who was murdered by her husband because she thought God valued her suffering, or the many who have left the church over disagreements with traditional theology),[37] perhaps this break can be seen positively. John Cobb says it well: "The fact that theologians once thought this way is no reason to think so now."[38] In fact, this break may well be liberating for many Christians struggling to make the traditional teachings they have received fit with their personal experiences of the world. And although this model is surely different from what early Anabaptist or Pietist theologians had in mind, it does share a point of connection with their demand that life be lived in imitation of Jesus.[39] But whereas these earlier theologians argued that a life of discipleship is a necessary *part* of salvation, this model argues that this balanced life *is* salvation. It is where we experience the closest contact with God. God's acting through us changes us and the world. As such, salvation must absolutely include a communal component. In this way, salvation looks different in this model than it does in most traditional theology.

Jesus' life models a vision that points to what salvation is like. This vision gives "humankind new vision to see the resources for positive, abundant relational life."[40] His example provides a clue for how to move beyond our own egocentrism. But Jesus need not be the only one who offers a model for how to achieve that abundant, relational life. This model of atonement does not necessitate that Jesus be God incarnate or the preexistent Son, both of which are exclusivist claims that are uncomfortable for many postmodern people. Instead, Jesus is a savior in that he offers an example to follow, and in this way, this model of atonement

37. See Borg, *Heart of Christianity*, xi–xii.

38. Cobb, *God and the World*, 91.

39. It is good and proper that contemporary Brethren theology should continue to grow and evolve while still maintaining a link to past emphases. For example, Gordon Kaufman warns that postmodern contexts and ways of thinking are so different from those of the sixteenth century that contemporary Anabaptists cannot indiscriminately implement these earlier ideas (Kaufman, *Context of Decision*, 9).

40. Williams, *Sisters in the Wilderness*, 165.

maintains close ties to traditional Anabaptist theology.[41] But there are other examples too. God offers a divine call for love and flourishing in many different ways. Some people may respond to God's invitation in the Buddha's call to live in the Middle Way. Perhaps this life between hedonism and extreme asceticism offers the best way for some to live in loving relationship to the rest of the cosmos. Or perhaps devotion to and participation in the love of Krishna is the clearest luring of God for others. The point is that Jesus was special in that he responded to God's luring in an incredible way that offers an authoritative example for millions of Christians,[42] but he is surely not the only one to respond to God in this way. And assuming that there must be life of some kind on other planets in the universe, beings there must also respond to God in ways that make the most sense for those kinds of life. Therefore, Jesus cannot possibly be the only means through which anyone or anything may access God; to believe so is to limit the creativity and imagination of God as well as to offer a hopelessly anthropocentric view of God, the universe, and salvation. Let us turn instead to a view of salvation that relies on a persuasive God who cares for all of creation, one that includes a social or communal element, and one that highlights care and concern for others as the determining factor in achieving salvation. This model offers an unusual (and even unorthodox) definition of salvation that prioritizes the global community over the individual.

Cooperative Salvation

Just as process thought re-imagined the concept of omnipotence, this model recommends that Brethren theology expand or re-imagine its

41. Walter Köhler argues that "with the Anabaptists the idea of justification is replaced by the idea of discipleship. Here Christ is an example or model rather than the 'savior'" (Köhler, *Dogmengeschichte*, 356, quoted in Friedmann, *Theology of Anabaptism*, 159).

42. We certainly should not discount the fact that Jesus is authoritative for many Christians, especially because Jesus' example is at the heart of Anabaptist theology. Marcus Borg offers a helpful way to think about why one would choose Christianity over another religion. He writes, "The Christian tradition is familiar; it is 'home' for me. I was born into it and grew up in it. Its stories, language, music, and ethos are familiar. It nurtured me, even as I have had to unlearn some of what I was taught" (Borg, *Heart of Christianity*, 223). Although there are harmful elements of Christian theology that must be relinquished, there is still much in this tradition that is meaningful, and it should not all be discarded.

concept of salvation. We must open ourselves to ideas of salvation that have nothing to do with eternal heavenly reward. I propose that Brethren prioritize social salvation (the transformation of the world's systems and structures to make them serve the least of these) over personal salvation—to the point that personal salvation only has meaning within a system of social transformation.

This model of salvation contains no heavenly, after-death reward for individual souls. Instead, it defines personal salvation as existing in right relationship with God, humanity, and all of creation *in this life*. Salvation is this-worldly; it changes the condition of all life on this planet. This does not mean that salvation brings an end to this earthly existence. It is neither an escape from the conditions of lived existence (heaven), nor an event that ushers in the end of time (eschaton). As Marcus Borg writes, salvation in the Bible "is not about the saving of individual souls for heaven, but about a new social and personal reality in the midst of this life."[43] Thus, this model recognizes the interconnectedness of those relationships such that none of the relationships can be right until they are all right. Therefore, for example, one cannot claim to be right with God (or "saved") when other people are starving to death and the planet is being wantonly polluted. In this way, the spiritual connection to God is directly related to the physical conditions on and of this Earth.[44] Thus, personal salvation is not just personal. It necessarily concerns others and their actions and relationships. For this reason, I label this model "cooperative salvation." Because salvation is *all* of creation in right relationship, no one is saved until everyone is saved.[45]

43. Ibid., 179.

44. Because this model of salvation is concerned for all of creation and this earthly existence, it necessarily includes a desire for environmental sustainability. Salvation is not an escape from this planet and its ecological problems. In fact, in order for salvation to be achieved, the planet itself must be nurtured.

45. This is not to deny that the possibility of individual salvation. Rather, this model seeks to address the split in much contemporary Christian theology between social and individual salvation. As J. Lawrence Burkholder observes, the contemporary church is split down the middle between those who see the church's function as bringing about the kingdom of God (social salvation) and those who see its function as saving souls (individual salvation). He finds that both are necessary for any meaningful ministry because the emphasis on individual salvation points to the need for "authentic existence in the face of ontological and moral alienation" while social salvation is concerned for justice and revolutionary change in the world (Burkholder, "People in Community," 6). He argues, "if the churches limit their task to one or the other, the Gospel is truncated, and the churches lose their point. Salvation is both individual and social. The churches must, therefore, find ways to express this fact both

Under the cooperative salvation model, social salvation is defined as the flourishing of all life in balance with other forms of life. This type of salvation changes the conditions of all life on the planet—not in a way that brings an end to this earthly existence, but in a way that decreases the amount of suffering in the world. To be sure, this type of social salvation will not bring all suffering to an end. Suffering is a part of our fragile and creaturely existence; death and suffering are creaturely realities that will not disappear.[46] However, when the conditions of social salvation are achieved, the suffering that results from power wielded over others will cease. When domination systems are dismantled and power is used *for* the good of others rather than *over* others in exploitation, the suffering of oppression will cease,[47] and life—both physical and spiritual—will flourish. Additionally, when all of creation is in communion with itself and with God, the intensity of the suffering that results from the creaturely realities of earthly existence (i.e., natural evil) will be diminished because it will be born communally rather than individually.

Although the model I am proposing here seems radically divorced from the Anabaptist norm, it does incorporate some important Anabaptist ideals, and it relies on the ideas of many of the theologians presented in this study. First and foremost, the cooperative salvation model takes Jesus' life and ministry seriously. In fact, the whole model is based on Jesus' care and concern for the physical needs of the least of these. Second, the cooperative salvation model draws on the traditional Anabaptist concern

---

theologically and practically" (ibid.).

I agree that both individual and communal elements are crucial to the biblical notion of salvation. However, I reject the notion that individual salvation is about saving souls. Instead, I view individual salvation as moments whereby individuals experience God's transformation of their own lives. For example, an alcoholic may experience salvation along his road to recovery as he repairs his life, his relationships, and his own body. However, this individual salvation is only one tiny piece of the whole of the salvation that is to come. This is not to deny the power and meaning one may find in an experience of individual salvation. It is merely to suggest that it is not the whole meaning of salvation.

46. Wendy Farley notes that even in traditional theology, redemption does not end the painfulness of our current, physical lives. See Farley, *Wounding and Healing*, 22.

47. Dorothee Söelle suggests that power that distributes itself to make others strong is good power (Söelle, *Silent Cry*, 158). This way of thinking about power may be quite helpful to Anabaptists who, as Burkholder correctly identifies, are wary of all situations that require the use of power rather than *agape* love. Through Söelle's linkage of power and love, these wary Anabaptists may be able to lay claim to (distributive) power and wield it for the good of others.

for the community.[48] From very early on in the movement, Anabaptists emphasized the importance of interpersonal relationships in connection with God. In fact, according to Robert Friedmann, Anabaptists believe that no one may come to God alone:

> All individualism and individualistic concern for personal salvation is ruled out. No one can enter the kingdom except together with his brother . . . The kingdom of God means from its very beginning a togetherness, else it is no kingdom. The mere aggregation of saved souls, as in Pietism, does not constitute the kingdom; it remains just an aggregation, nothing else. The horizontal man-to-man relationship belongs to the kingdom just as much as does the vertical God-man relationship. In fact, the belief prevails that one cannot come to God (that is, attain salvation) except as one comes to Him together with one's brother.[49]

The cooperative salvation model explicitly states that no one can attain salvation alone. In this way, it reclaims an important element of Anabaptist soteriology that was obscured by the influence of fundamentalism and its emphasis on personal salvation.

Third, this model is concerned primarily with the here and now. Anabaptists have always insisted that the present situation in life matters. Arnold Snyder describes it this way:

> Central to the Anabaptist understanding of Christ's satisfaction for sin, then, is not simply 'believing' that the saving act happened historically and 'believing' that the historical atonement applies to the forgiveness of one's personal sin, but further, there must be a 'proving' of the already-accomplished redemption by means of concrete response and action. Redemption is not simply about sins being forgiven in heaven (although it is about that); it is also about the cessation of actual sin, here and now.[50]

48. Scott Holland notes that Anabaptists have often viewed the community as the privileged and only proper theological reality (Holland, "Communal Hermeneutics," 101). This epistemological claim can be insulating and constricting, as Holland points out, but communal hermeneutics (perhaps only in an ideal form) can also guard against the notion that salvation has only to do with the individual.

49. Friedmann, "Doctrine of the Two Worlds," 112–13.

50. Snyder, *Following in the Footsteps*, 54. Similarly, Willard Swartley argues that especially in John's Gospel, eternal life is not so much about a future experience as it is about a here-and-now experience of newness and transformed living freed from sin (Swartley, *Covenant of Peace*, 315). Likewise, Friedmann argues, "these men and women knew themselves to be redeemed persons who had achieved a certain consciousness of salvation or divine grace in the here and now. They felt as if they were

Though the cooperative salvation model highlights this here-and-now aspect of salvation, it differs from traditional Anabaptist soteriology in that it completely ignores the possibility of a heavenly reward.[51] There are several benefits to disregarding the hereafter. Most importantly, it values material bodies in this world. Models of salvation that promise heavenly reward usually perpetuate the centuries-long Christian practice of valuing the spiritual over the material. In so doing, they esteem the knowledge and experience of the rich (because only those who are well fed and comfortable can ignore their bodies) and men (as the gender not usually associated with "natural," bodily functions).[52] Thus, by focusing on the physical bodies of those on this planet (as well as the body of the planet itself), this model of cooperative salvation upsets the value hierarchy of the spirit/matter dualism and is especially concerned with the experiences and insights of those often condemned and marginalized as too concerned with the material stuff of bodies.

---

already in God's womb; hence they were no longer worried about man's constitutive corruption and lostness. If they were otherwise, they might rejoin, how could God ask man to *obey* His command and not be a disciple?" (Friedmann, *Theology of Anabaptism*, 32–33).

51. Although this model eliminates all hope for a heavenly reward, it does not reject the possibility of life after death. Knowledge of such matters is surely beyond any human's capabilities. However, I have removed all speculation about heaven (and what a believer must do to get into heaven) from this model because it seems to make Christians ignore the needs of others in this life. For example, it is my sense that Anabaptists' desire to maintain moral purity by refusing political participation is fueled, at least in part, by the desire for personal salvation. Although Anabaptists across generations have written about and discussed the need to be separated from the world in terms of being obedient to Jesus' example and God's will, it seems that the primary underlying reasoning for this obedience is to collect some kind of personal reward in heaven. Surely this is not the only reason Anabaptists desire to be obedient, but I wonder if that possibility were removed outright, whether many contemporary Anabaptists would cling as tightly to the idea of complete separation from the world.

52. May, *Body Knows*, 18. I deeply appreciate May's reclamation of the body (especially the female body) as a source for theological reflection as well as her notion of corporate, "practiced" resurrection. In contrast to many theories of resurrection, May's model does not denigrate earthly bodies (as inferior to spiritual bodies), nor does it limit resurrection to individuals' after-death experiences. For example, she writes, "This Good News comes to me in the way it came to those to whom Jesus made it known: it is announced by bodies—by bodies fed and clothed and touched, by bodies freed from chains, by bodies healed. Accordingly, I believe the resurrection of the body—which, in turn transfigures the mind—happens whenever and wherever we participate in a new solidarity with and presence to our own bodies and the bodies of others. Resurrection happens as we are incorporated into the body of the Risen One as we honor as holy 'the body of God,' i.e., the earth" (ibid., 104).

Models of salvation that promise a life after death free from all the suffering and travails of life also tend to minimize the real pain of suffering in this life. Under these models, suffering is to be patiently endured in the manner of Jesus. These models encourage those who suffer to remain in their distressing situations, relieving others of any responsibility to change those situations for the better. Because this whole model of cooperative salvation depends upon alleviating suffering for all, it especially highlights the responsibility Christians have to change these situations on behalf of their sisters and brothers around the world. It assumes that if human beings are saved *in* this world rather than out of it, then they will surely be more invested in caring for this world and those in it.

Fourth, this model rests on the optimistic theological anthropology of the early Anabaptists. It presumes that humanity is originally created good. This "natural knowledge of the good"[53] grants us a role to play in the process of salvation: we must work at righting relationships and dismantling worldly structures that contribute to suffering. However, we are also dependent upon the support and guidance of God's persuasive lure to restore that original goodness.[54] In Cynthia Crysdale's terms, we must make use of operative grace, those "aha!" moments where we suddenly see opportunities for improved relationship.[55] This seems to be the same idea that process theology has in mind when it describes the way God lures us toward positive action, or what Marcus Borg describes as "thin

53. Klassen, *Covenant and Community*, 111.

54. The early Anabaptists assumed that it was the Spirit that granted enabling grace and guided disciples in paths of radical discipleship. In this way, their optimistic hope for human perfection (that humans can actually follow Jesus' commandments) was less a confidence in human capabilities and more a faith in the power of the Holy Spirit (Snyder, *Sattler*, 168). This reminder is crucial for Anabaptists who think they will lose their actual righteousness (and their salvation) through compromise with the world in the form of political participation. Although they may not consciously acknowledge it, this insistence on remaining separated from the world to keep their hands and souls clean underestimates the power of the Spirit. If the enabling Spirit can redeem and transform sinners into radical disciples on their way to perfection, surely it is also powerful enough to redeem parts of the world through the actions of disciples. Barbara Nelson Gingerich offers a valid criticism when she points out that not all people are naturally inclined to work for peace and justice. She argues that some kind of conversion or redemption must occur in order for some people to be open to this goal (Gingerich, "Radical Pacifism," 50). I agree that some people will need to be pushed harder by the Spirit to move away from the self-obsessed way of life than others will be, but that push—or conversion experience—does not encompass the entirety of salvation.

55. Crysdale, *Embracing Travail*, 33–37.

places."[56] These are instances where the will of the divine breaks through our worldly consciousness and makes itself clear to us. Once we have had such an experience, we become aware of God's presence in the world and in ourselves, so that even after the memory starts to fade, we cannot dismiss the knowledge that God wills something specific for the world. This lingering (perhaps subconscious) knowledge pushes us to try to discern God's will and work to make it so in the world. There is something about this mystical experience that causes us to work to keep from falling back into a permanent state of egocentrism or sin.

In this model, salvation is not a matter of forgiveness for human sin; it is about the transformation of the world. It draws on sixteenth-century Anabaptist theologian Balthasar Hubmaier's understanding of God's enabling grace. Unlike some of his Anabaptist contemporaries, who defined grace as the power of God by which one is reborn and restored to the image of God (or divinized), Hubmaier understood grace as the power of God to restore humanity's ability to choose and do good.[57] This idea seems remarkably similar to the idea in process theology that God lures humanity to choose the good. When disciples respond positively to this lure, they gain the perspective and vision necessary to see the possibilities of a transformed world. In this way, believers who work for cooperative salvation are buoyed and directed by God. Although disciples' actions remain human actions, they are informed by the spirit of God and the character of Jesus' example.[58]

56. Borg, *Heart of Christianity*, 155–56.

57. Mabry, *Balthasar Hubmaier's Doctrine*, 112.

58. This model of cooperative salvation does not depend on a blend of Anabaptist and Protestant soteriology alone. It also relies on what others outside of the Anabaptist tradition are doing, thinking, and writing about in terms of social justice from a theological perspective. Much of Anabaptist theology tends to be fairly insular because it is suspicious that all those outside of Anabaptism have succumbed to Constantinian temptation and do not maintain adequate distinction between the church and the world. However, the model of cooperative salvation eases this tension with other Christians and allows for greater partnering with those outside of the Anabaptist tradition. Actively engaging the world's systems and structures is fairly new territory for contemporary Anabaptists, so they must depend on some of the work that those in other denominations have done regarding the church's relationship to the world. A full examination of these other views of church and world is, of course, outside the scope of this project. However, it is my sense that many contemporary Anabaptists are quite sympathetic to the theologies written by (or for) those on the underside of history. They appreciate the theories proposed by various liberation theologies and postcolonial theologies, but they do not embrace their practical or political implications, because to do so would involve compromising their nonviolent ethics. Given

This constructive model still maintains a role for the visible church as the gathered body of believers that is directed by God's spirit to work in the world for social salvation. It also retains some form of the two-kingdom doctrine of traditional Anabaptist theology in that it maintains a distinction between church and world. But what makes the church community distinct from the rest of the world is not that it is composed only of redeemed individuals or only of those who follow literally Jesus' teachings and commands.[59] Instead, what separates the church from the world is that its members are working for the good of the entire world.[60] They are the ones who are engaging the world for the benefits of others rather than for any immediate benefit to themselves. They may not follow exactly Jesus' methods, but they do embody his concern for others. The members of the visible church recognize that domination systems

---

that the cooperative salvation model eases the restrictions of political action, perhaps contemporary Anabaptists now have the theological justification to fully engage those theologies and their political goals.

59. After all, those inside the church are also fallible. Elaine Swartzentruber correctly cautions contemporary Anabaptists to be realistic about the limitations of the church. Although early Anabaptists claimed a transcendent authority for the community as the body of Christ, Swartzentruber warns that the body is always embodied and contextual. Therefore, they cannot "claim a transcendent authority for decisions we make, for lines we draw, for people we include or exclude from our fellowship, [or] for the lines we will not cross," but instead must "acknowledge that we overlay the politics of our times—our violence, loss, longing, love, desire and fears—on the claimed transcendent body of Christ, whether it be in the way we read Scriptures, the way we choose leaders or the way we work in the world. An Embodied Body of Christ, incarnated into the real world, takes on the lines of power and the functions of power in the world. As such we cannot claim a special dispensation of purity, nor demand such a dispensation. We must acknowledge that the lines of purity and authority that we draw in good faith are always human, always fallible, always contextual, contingent and contested and must never be claimed as anything else" (Swartzentruber, "Marking and Remarking," 264).

60. Arnold Snyder and John Rempel both worry that contemporary Anabaptist theology is moving in the direction of magisterial Protestant or Constantinian theology, in which the two kingdoms that oppose one another are not church and world, but the internal/private and external/public (Rempel, "Ambiguous Legacy," 362; Snyder, *Anabaptist History and Theology*, 423). Although I am proposing a soteriological model that advocates political or worldly engagement, the distinction I make between church and world (or religion and politics) is not a matter of separating public and private. Instead, this distinction is on the level of motive. Those who are committed to the visible church and to working towards social salvation will not affirm every single political action. Instead, they must discern life-giving systems and actions from those that are death-dealing. For a more detailed argument of this point, see Eisenbise, *For Thy Neighbors' Good*, 162–68.

continue to operate in full force in our world, but like Walter Wink, they acknowledge that at times these structures are the most effective, useful ways to care for the least. For, as Mennonite theologian J. Lawrence Burkholder writes, "The political order is not the Kingdom of God, and of course, neither is the church . . . But a lot can be done in the political sphere without Kingdom pretensions, that points in the direction of the Kingdom of God."[61]

Salvation entails right relationship with God and all of creation. Therefore, it is necessarily an ongoing process. Salvation cannot possibly be a once-and-done event; it involves constantly working at these relationships and being aware of how our actions affect God and the world. Instead of depending on God to swoop in and fix everything that is wrong in the world, this model relies on humanity discerning the will of God and working to live out that will in the world. God is at work in us, goading us out of situations of isolation and towards right relationship, towards acting out the divine will for us, for the world, and for our salvation. God is at work in the world effecting our salvation, not through supernatural intervention, but by persuading the actions of faithful people. There will never be a time when God finally decides to end evil once and for all by plunging to earth to put everything right again. Instead, salvation will be achieved once everyone responds to God's persuasive call to choose the good. The good news of Christianity is that God cares deeply and intimately for us and wants what is best for us. Wendy Farley captures this idea poetically: "Egocentrism whispered the despairing lie that we are alone. But as the isolation of egocentrism breaks down, the deep intimacy we share with the Beloved and through the Beloved with every being becomes part of our lived experience."[62] But as Jon Sobrino points out, Jesus (and God) are not equally for everyone.[63] What is best for some might be that they lose their own power and glory so that others may gain dignity. There cannot be a once-and-done solution to the human problem of isolation and self-absorption because it has so many different and contextual manifestations. The work of salvation falls on

---

61. Burkholder, "Autobiographical Reflections," 46. He adds that over his lifetime, he "learned that the political realm could offer an avenue for delivering a lot of this world's goods to alleviate suffering" (ibid., 13). For a complete discussion of how the church can partner with worldly systems for the benefit of those who suffer, see Eisenbise, *For Thy Neighbors' Good*, 162–68.

62. Farley, *Wounding and Healing*, 34.

63. Sobrino, *Jesus the Liberator*, 79.

us. We must discern the best way to follow Jesus' example of fighting the domination system in our own contexts. Only then will salvation begin to be realized.

We now come full circle and return to the question that began this book: "What does it mean that Jesus died for my sins?" According to this model, the answer is that Jesus did not die for my sins. Jesus—and many others—died *because of* my sins and those of other people who are trapped in and benefit from the domination system. Jesus died because he opposed the domination system at every turn, and it killed him because he was a threat. Jesus' death is not special in that it changed the relationship between humanity and God or that it revealed something about God's ultimate plan for the world. Jesus' death is typical in that those who resist the powers of domination are killed. There are countless examples of this heartbreaking fact, and Jesus' death is no more tragic than any of these other deaths. But Jesus' life and ministry are special in that they give us an inspiring example of what it looks like to accept God's invitation to act for the flourishing of all. This, then, is the seed of salvation, and it is up to all of us to nourish that seedling until full social salvation is achieved.

Bibliography

Abelard, Peter. *Commentary on the Epistle to the Romans.* Translated by Steven R. Cartwright. Fathers of the Church: Mediaeval Continuation 12. Washington, DC: Catholic University of America Press, 2011.

Anselm, Saint, Archbishop of Canterbury. *Why God Became Man, and the Virgin Conception and Original Sin.* Translated by Joseph M. Colleran. Albany, NY: Magi, 1969.

Athanasius, Saint, Patriarch of Alexandria. *On the Incarnation.* Translated by John Behr. Popular Patristics 44b. Crestwood, NY: Saint Vladimir's Seminary Press, 2011.

Augustine, Saint, Bishop of Hippo. *Confessions.* Translated by R. S. Pine-Coffin. Penguin Classics L114. New York: Penguin, 1961.

Aulén, Gustav. *Christus Victor: An Historical Study of the Three Main Types of the Idea of Atonement.* Translated by A. G. Herbert. New York: Macmillan, 1969.

Baker, Sharon L. "By Grace? An 'Economy' of Atonement." PhD diss., Southern Methodist University, 2006.

Bender, Harold S. "The Anabaptist Vision." *Mennonite Quarterly Review* 18 (1944) 67–88.

Berkhof, Hendrik. *Christ and the Powers.* Translated by John Howard Yoder. Scottdale, PA: Herald, 1962.

Birch, Bruce C., et al. *A Theological Introduction to the Old Testament.* Nashville: Abingdon, 1999.

Borg, Marcus J. "Executed by Rome, Vindicated by God." In *Stricken by God? Nonviolent Identification and the Victory of Christ,* edited by Brad Jersak and Michael Hardin, 150–65. Grand Rapids: Eerdmans, 2007.

———. *The Heart of Christianity: Rediscovering a Life of Faith.* New York: HarperSanFrancisco, 2003.

Bowman, Carl Desportes. *Portrait of a People: The Church of the Brethren at 300.* Elgin, IL: Brethren, 2008.

Brock, Rita Nakashima, and Rebecca Ann Parker. *Proverbs of Ashes: Violence, Redemptive Suffering, and the Search for What Saves Us.* Boston: Beacon, 2001.

Brown, Dale W. *Understanding Pietism.* Rev. ed. Nappanee, IN: Evangel, 1996.

Brown, Joanne Carlson, and Rebecca Parker. "For God So Loved the World?" In *Christianity, Patriarchy, and Abuse: A Feminist Critique,* edited by Joanne Carlson Brown and Carole R. Bohn, 1–30. New York: Pilgrim, 1989.

Budry, Edmund L. "Thine Is the Glory." In *Hymnal: A Worship Book*, edited by Rebecca Slough, 269. Elgin, IL: Brethren, 1992.

Burkholder, John Lawrence. "A People in Community—Contemporary Relevance." *Mennonite Life* (1968) 5–12.

———. "Autobiographical Reflections." In *The Limits of Perfection: A Conversation with J. Lawrence Burkholder*, edited by Rodney J. Sawatsky and Scott Holland, 1–54. Kitchener, Canada: Pandora, 1993.

Calvin, John. *Institutes of the Christian Religion*. Translated by Henry Beveridge. Peabody, MA: Hendrickson, 2008.

Cecil, Everett Leo. "Rauschenbusch's Concept of Man and Salvation." MA diss., Pacific School of Religion, 1957.

Church of the Brethren. *Minutes of the Annual Meetings of the Brethren*. Dayton, OH: Christian Publishing Association, 1876.

Cobb, John B., Jr. *God and the World*. Eugene, OR: Wipf & Stock, 2000.

Cobb, John B., Jr., and David Ray Griffin. *Process Theology: An Introductory Exposition*. Louisville: Westminster John Knox, 1976.

Cone, James H. *God of the Oppressed*. Rev. ed. Maryknoll, NY: Orbis, 1997.

Crysdale, Cynthia S. W. *Embracing Travail: Retrieving the Cross Today*. New York: Continuum, 1999.

Cyprian, Saint, Bishop of Carthage. *The Writings of Cyprian, Bishop of Carthage*. Translated by Robert Ernest Wallace. Ante-Nicene Christian Library 1. Edinburgh: T. & T. Clark, 1882.

Deppermann, Klaus, and Benjamin Drewery. *Melchior Hoffman: Social Unrest and Apocalyptic Visions in the Age of Reformation*. Edinburgh: T. & T. Clark, 1987.

Durnbaugh, Donald F. *The Believers' Church: The History and Character of Radical Protestantism*. Eugene, OR: Wipf & Stock, 2003.

———. *Fruit of the Vine: A History of the Brethren, 1708–1995*. Elgin, IL: Brethren, 1997.

Durnbaugh, Donald F., and Carl Desportes Bowman. *Church of the Brethren: Yesterday and Today*. Elgin, IL: Brethren, 1986.

Eisenbise, Kathryn S. "Come to the Table: Meals and Table Fellowship from the Jesus Movement to the Eucharist." MDiv diss., Bethany Theological Seminary, 2004.

———. *For Thy Neighbors' Good: Anabaptist Soteriology, Separatism, and Social Salvation; A Dissertation*. Ann Arbor, MI: ProQuest, 2009.

———. "Resurrection as Victory? The Eschatological Implications of J. Denny Weaver's 'Narrative Christus Victor' Model of Atonement." *Brethren Life and Thought* 53 (2008) 9–22.

Eller, Vernard. *Kierkegaard and Radical Discipleship: A New Perspective*. Princeton, NJ: Princeton University Press, 1968.

Farley, Wendy. *The Wounding and Healing of Desire: Weaving Heaven and Earth*. Louisville: Westminster John Knox 2005.

Finger, Thomas N. *A Contemporary Anabaptist Theology: Biblical, Historical, Constructive*. Downers Grove, IL: InterVarsity, 2004.

———. "*Christus Victor* as Nonviolent Atonement." *Atonement and Violence: A Theological Conversion*, edited by John Sanders, 87–114. Nashville: Abingdon, 2006.

Foley, George Cadwalader. *Anselm's Theory of Atonement*. London: Longmans, Green, 1909. University of Toronto Libraries, https://archive.org/details/anselmstheoryoofoleuoft.

Ford, Lewis S. "Divine Persuasion and the Triumph of Good." In *Process Philosophy and Christian Thought*, edited by Delwin Brown, et al., 287–304. New York: Bobbs-Merrill, 1971.

Friedmann, Robert. "The Doctrine of the Two Worlds." In *The Recovery of the Anabaptist Vision: A Sixtieth Anniversary Tribute to Harold S. Bender*, edited by Guy F. Hershberger, 105–118. Scottdale, PA: Herald, 1957.

———. "On Mennonite Historiography and on Individualism and Brotherhood: A Communication from Dr. Robert Friedmann." *Mennonite Quarterly Review* 18 (1944) 117–22.

———. *The Theology of Anabaptism: An Interpretation*. Scottdale, PA: Herald, 1973.

Gibson, Mel, et al. *The Passion of the Christ*. Directed by Mel Gibson. 2004. Beverly Hills, CA: 20th Century Fox Home Entertainment, 2004. DVD.

Gillon, Campbell. *Words to Trust*. Women Writers Series. Edinburgh: T. & T. Clark, 1991.

Gingerich, Barbara Nelson. "Radical Pacifism." In *Mennonite Peace Theology: A Panorama of Types*, edited by John Richard Burkholder and Barbara Nelson Gingerich, 42–51. Akron, PA: Mennonite Central Committee Peace Office, 1991.

Gonález, Justo L. *Christian Thought Revisited: Three Types of Theology*. Nashville: Abingdon, 1989.

Gordon, Ronald J. "Pietism and the Brethren in Seventeenth-century Germany." *Church of the Brethren Network*. Last modified November 2011. http://www.cob-net.org/pietism.htm.

Green, Joel B., and Mark D. Baker. *Recovering the Scandal of the Cross: Atonement in New Testament and Contemporary Contexts*. Downers Grove, IL: InterVarsity, 2000.

Gregory, Saint of Nyssa. "The Great Catechism." In *Gregory of Nyssa: Dogmatic Treatises, etc.* Vol. 5 of *The Nicene and Post-Nicene Fathers*, Series 2, edited by Philip Schaff Gregory et al., 473–509. Peabody, MA: Hendrickson, 1994.

Gutiérrez, Gustavo. *A Theology of Liberation: History, Politics, and Salvation*. Rev. ed. Maryknoll, NY: Orbis, 1988.

Hauerwas, Stanley. "The Testament of Friends." *Christian Century* 107 (1990) 212–16.

Heilke, Thomas. "Yoder's Idea of Constantinianism: An Analytical Framework Toward Conversation." In *A Mind Patient and Untamed: Assessing John Howard Yoder's Contributions to Theology, Ethics, and Peacemaking*, edited by Gayle Gerber Koontz and Ben C. Ollenburger, 89–125. Telford, PA: Cascadia, 2004.

Herzog, Frederick. *European Pietism Reviewed*. Princeton Theological Monograph Series. San Jose, CA: Pickwick, 2003.

Hodge, Charles. *Systematic Theology*. Vol. 2. Grand Rapids: Eerdmans, 1952.

Holland, Scott. "Communal Hermeneutics as Body Politics or Disembodied Theology?" *Brethren Life and Thought* 40 (1995) 94–110.

———. "The Gospel of Peace and the Violence of God." In *Seeking Cultures of Peace: A Peace Church Conversation*, edited by Fernando Enns et al., 132–46. Telford, PA: Cascadia, 2004.

Huebner, Chris K. "Mennonites and Narrative Theology: The Case of John Howard Yoder." *The Conrad Grebel Review* 16 (1998) 15–38.

Irenaeus, Saint, Bishop of Lyons. *Five Books of St. Irenaeus, Bishop of Lyons, Against Heresies*. Translated by John Keble. Library of Fathers of the Holy Catholic Church 42. Oxford: Parker, 1872.

Jennings, John, et al. *Two Discourses: The First, of Preaching Christ; The Second, of Particular and Experimental Preaching*. Edinburgh: Campbell & Wallace, 1793.

Jersak, Brad, and Michael Hardin, eds. *Stricken by God? Nonviolent Identification and the Victory of Christ*. Grand Rapids: Eerdmans, 2007.

Kaufman, Gordon D. *The Context of Decision: A Theological Analysis*. Menno Simons Lectures 1959. New York: Abingdon, 1961.

———. *In Face of Mystery: A Constructive Theology*. Cambridge: Harvard University Press, 1993.

Keeney, Jonathan B. *Church of the Brethren Annual Conference Minutes, 1778–2004, Topical Index*. Elgin, IL: Church of the Brethren General Board, 2005. http://www.brethren.org/bhla/documents/index-to-annual-conference-minutes.pdf.

King, Martin Luther, Jr. "Suffering and Faith." In *A Testament of Hope: The Essential Writings and Speeches of Martin Luther King, Jr.*, 41–42, edited by James Melvin Washington. New York: HarperOne, 1991.

Klassen, William. *Covenant and Community: The Life, Writings, and Hermeneutics of Pilgram Marpeck*. Grand Rapids: Eerdmans, 1968.

Köhler, Walther. *Dogmengeschichte: als Geschichte des Christlichen Selbstbewusstseins, das Zeitalter der Reformation*. Zurich: Niehan, 1951.

Koontz, Gayle Gerber. "Confessional Theology in a Pluralistic Context: A Study of the Theological Ethics of H. Richard Niebuhr and John H. Yoder." PhD diss., Boston University, 1985.

Kostlevy, William. Introduction to *Theological Writings on Various Subjects*, by Peter Nead, i–vii. Youngstown, OH: Dunker Springhaus Ministries, 1997.

Kraus, C. Norman. *God Our Savior: Theology in a Christological Mode*. Scottdale, PA: Herald, 1991.

———. *Jesus Christ Our Lord: Christology from a Disciple's Perspective*. Scottdale, PA: Herald, 1987.

Kraybill, Donald B. *The Upside-down Kingdom*. 25th anniv. ed. Scottdale, PA: Herald, 2003.

Kraybill, Donald B., and Kathryn Eisenbise. *The Brethren in a Postmodern World*. Perspectives Essay Series. Elgin, IL: Brethren, 2006.

Love, Gregory Anderson. *Love, Violence, and the Cross: How the Nonviolent God Saves us through the Cross of Christ*. Eugene, OR: Cascade, 2010.

Lowry, Robert. "Low in the Grave He Lay." In *Hymnal: A Worship Book*, edited by Rebecca Slough, 273. Elgin, IL: Brethren, 1992.

Luther, Martin. "Let Your Sins Be Strong: A Letter from Luther to Melanchthon." In vol. 15 of *Dr. Martin Luther's Saemmtliche Schriften*, edited by Johann Georg Walch and translated by Erika Bullman Flores, n.p. Saint Louis: Concordia, n.d. http://www.iclnet.org/pub/resources/text/wittenberg/luther/letsinsbe.txt.

Lyman, Rebecca J. *Christology and Cosmology: Models of Divine Activity in Origen, Eusebius, and Athanasius*. Oxford Theological Monographs. Oxford: Clarendon, 1993.

Mabry, Eddie Louis. *Balthasar Hubmaier's Doctrine of the Church*. Lanham, MD: University Press of America, 1994.

Mack, Alexander. "Basic Questions." In *The Complete Writings of Alexander Mack.* Edited by William R. Eberly. Winona Lake, IN: BMH, 1991.

Marshall, Christopher D. "Atonement, Violence, and the Will of God: A Sympathetic Response to J. Denny Weaver's *The Nonviolent Atonement.*" *Mennonite Quarterly Review* 77 (2003) 69–92.

Martens, Peter W. "The Quest for an Anabaptist Atonement: Violence and Nonviolence in J. Denny Weaver's *The Nonviolent Atonement.*" *Mennonite Quarterly Review* 82 (2008) 281–311.

May, Melanie. *A Body Knows: A Theopoetics of Death and Resurrection.* New York: Continuum, 1995.

McClendon, James William, Jr. *Doctrine.* Vol. 2 of *Systematic Theology.* Nashville: Abingdon, 1994.

McFague, Sallie. *The Body of God: An Ecological Theology.* Minneapolis: Fortress, 1993.

McGrath, Alister E. *Christian Literature: An Anthology.* Oxford: Blackwell, 2001.

McIntyre, John. *The Shape of Soteriology: Studies in the Doctrine of the Death of Christ.* Edinburgh: T. & T. Clark, 2000.

Meier, Marcus. "The Brethren: A Church between Anabaptism and Pietism." In *Celebrating a Past, Envisioning a Future: The Fourth Brethren World Assembly and the 300th Anniversary Celebration, Schwarzenau, Germany, August 2–3, 2008*, edited by Dale R. Stoffer, 111–28. Philadelphia: Brethren Encyclopedia, 2009.

Mesle, C. Robert. *Process Theology: A Basic Introduction.* Saint Louis: Chalice, 1993.

Moltmann, Jürgen. *The Crucified God: The Cross of Christ as the Foundation and Criticism of Christian Theology.* Minneapolis: Fortress, 1993.

———. "The Crucified God: Yesterday and Today (1972–2002)." In *Cross Examinations: Readings on the Meaning of the Cross Today*, edited by Marit Trelstad, 127–38. Minneapolis: Fortress, 2006.

———. *Theology of Hope: On the Ground and Implications of a Christian Eschatology.* Minneapolis: Fortress, 1993.

Moore, Sebastian. *The Crucified Is No Stranger.* London: Darton, Longman, & Todd, 1977.

Nagler, Arthur Wilford. *Pietism and Methodism.* Nashville: Methodist Episcopal Church South, 1918.

Nation, Mark. *John Howard Yoder: Mennonite Patience, Evangelical Witness, Catholic Convictions.* Grand Rapids: Eerdmans, 2006.

Nead, Peter. *Theological Writings on Various Subjects.* Youngstown, OH: Dunker Springhaus Ministries, 1997.

Novak, David. "The Covenant in Rabbinic Thought." In *Two Faiths, One Covenant? Jewish and Christian Identity in the Presence of the Other*, edited by Eugene B. Korn and John T. Pawlikowski, 65–80. Bernardin Center Series. Lanham, MD: Sheed & Ward, 2004.

O'Collins, Gerald. *Interpreting Jesus.* Introducing Catholic Theology 2. Ramsey, NJ: Paulist, 1983.

Placher, William C. *Narratives of a Vulnerable God: Christ, Theology, and Scripture.* Louisville: Westminster John Knox, 1994.

Plaskow, Judith. *Sex, Sin, and Grace: Women's Experience and the Theologies of Reinhold Niebuhr and Paul Tillich.* Lanham, MD: University Press of America, 1980.

Prothero, Stephen R. *God Is Not One: The Eight Rival Religions That Run the World—and Why Their Differences Matter.* New York: HarperOne, 2010.

Rauschenbusch, Walter. *Christianizing the Social Order*. Boston: Pilgrim, 1912.

———. *A Theology for the Social Gospel*. Nashville: Abingdon, 1945.

Reesor-Taylor, Rachel. "Yoder's Mischievous Contribution to Mennonite Views on Anselmian Atonement." In *A Mind Patient and Untamed*, edited by Ben C. Ollenburger and Gayle Gerber Koontz, 303–317. Telford, PA: Cascadia, 2004.

Reimarus, Hermann S. *Reimarus: Fragments*. Edited by Charles H. Talbert and translated by Ralph S. Fraser. Lives of Jesus Series. Philadelphia: Fortress, 1970.

Reimer, A. James. *Mennonites and Classical Theology: Dogmatic Foundations for Christian Ethics*. Kitchener, Canada: Pandora, 2001.

Rempel, John D. "Ambiguous Legacy: The Peace Teaching, Speaking Truth to Power, and Mennonite Assimilation through the Centuries." In *At Peace and Unafraid: Public Order, Security, and the Wisdom of the Cross*, edited by Duane K. Friesen and Gerald W. Schlabach, 349–63. Scottdale, PA: Herald, 2005.

Robertson, Archibald. Introduction to *Athanasius de Incarnatione*, by Saint Athanasius, ix–xxiv. Translated by Archibald Robertson. 2nd ed. London: D. Nutt, 1891.

Ruether, Rosemary Radford. *Sexism and God-Talk: Toward a Feminist Theology*. Boston: Beacon, 1993.

Sawatsky, Rodney J. "John Howard Yoder (1927–)." In *Nonviolence—Central to Christian Spirituality: Perspectives from Scripture to the Present*, edited by Joseph T. Culliton, 239–69. Toronto Studies in Theology 8. New York: Mellen, 1982.

Sawatsky, Rodney J., and Scott Holland, eds. *The Limits of Perfection: A Conversation with J. Lawrence Burkholder*. Kitchener, Canada: Pandora, 1993.

Schertz, Mary H. "God's Cross and Women's Questions: A Biblical Perspective on Atonement." *Mennonite Quarterly Review* 68 (1994) 194–208.

Schmiechen, Peter. *Saving Power: Theories of Atonement and Forms of the Church*. Grand Rapids: Eerdmans, 2005.

Schüssler Fiorenza, Elisabeth. *In Memory of Her: A Feminist Theological Reconstruction of Christian Origins*. 10th anniv. ed. New York: Crossroad, 2002.

Simons, Menno. *A Foundation and Plain Instruction of the Saving Doctrine of Our Lord Jesus Christ*. Translated by I. Daniel Rupp. Lancaster, PA: Herr, 1835.

Snyder, C. Arnold. *Anabaptist History and Theology: An Introduction*. Kitchener, Canada: Pandora, 1995.

———. *Following in the Footsteps of Christ: The Anabaptist Tradition*. Maryknoll, NY: Orbis, 2004.

———. *The Life and Thought of Michael Sattler*. Scottdale, PA: Herald, 1984.

Sobrino, Jon. *Jesus the Liberator: A Historical-theological Reading of Jesus of Nazareth*. Translated by Paul Burns and Francis McDonagh. Maryknoll, NY: Orbis, 2004.

Söelle, Dorothee. *The Silent Cry: Mysticism and Resistance*. Minneapolis: Fortress, 2001.

———. *Suffering*. Translated by Everett R. Kalin. Philadelphia: Fortress, 1975.

Spener, Philipp Jakob. *Pia Desideria*. Translated and edited by Theodore G. Tappert. 1675. Reprint, Philadelphia: Fortress, 1964.

Sproul, R. C. *Essential Truths of the Christian Faith*. Wheaton, IL: Tyndale, 1992.

Stoffer, Dale R. "A Swiss Brethren (Anabaptist) Source for the Beliefs of Alexander Mack and the Early Brethren." *Brethren Life and Thought* 48 (2003) 29–38.

Strayer, James M., et al. "From Monogenesis to Polygenesis." *Mennonite Quarterly Review* 49 (1975) 83–121.

Swartley, Willard M. *Covenant of Peace: The Missing Peace in New Testament Theology and Ethics*. Grand Rapids: Eerdmans, 2006.

Swartzentruber, Elaine K. "Marking and Remarking the Body of Christ: Toward a Postmodern Mennonite Ecclesiology." *Mennonite Quarterly Review* 71 (1997) 243–65.

Talbert, Charles H. Introduction to *Reimarus: Fragments*, by Hermann S. Reimarus, 29–43. Edited by Charles H. Talbert and translated by Ralph S. Fraser. Philadelphia: Fortress, 1970.

Tertullian. "Against the Jews." In *Latin Christianity: Its Founder Tertullian*. Vol. 3 of *Ante-Nicene Fathers: The Writings of the Fathers down to AD 325*, edited by Alexander Roberts and James Donaldson, 151–74. Peabody, MA: Hendrickson, 1995.

Weaver, J. Denny. "Christus Victor, Ecclesiology, and Christology." *Mennonite Quarterly Review* 68 (1994) 272–90.

———. *Keeping Salvation Ethical: Mennonite and Amish Atonement Theory in the Late Nineteenth Century*. Studies in Anabaptist and Mennonite History 35. Scottdale, PA: Herald, 1997.

———. "Narrative *Christus Victor*: The Answer to Anselmian Atonement Violence." In *Atonement and Violence: A Theological Conversation*, edited by John Sanders, 1–32. Nashville: Abingdon, 2006.

———. *The Nonviolent Atonement*. Grand Rapids: Eerdmans, 2001.

———. "Peace-Shaped Theology." In *A Tribute to John Howard Yoder*, by John Howard Yoder, 22–28. Faith and Freedom 5. Bentley, Australia: Faith and Freedom, 1996.

———. "Reading the Past, Present, and Future in Revelation." In *Apocalypticism and Millennialism: Shaping a Believers Church Eschatology for the Twenty-First Century*, edited by Loren L. Johns, 97–112. Studies in the Believers Church Tradition 2. Kitchener, Canada: Pandora, 2000.

———. "Some Theological Implications of Christus Victor," *Mennonite Quarterly Review* 68 (1994) 483–99.

Weber, Max. *Protestant Ethic and the Spirit of Capitalism*. Translated by Talcott Parsons. New York: Scribner, 1958.

Weingart, Richard E. *The Logic of Divine Love: A Critical Analysis of the Soteriology of Peter Abailard*. London: Clarendon, 1970.

Wildenhahn, Carl August. *Philipp Jacob Spener: A Historical Life Picture*. Edited by J. K. Shryock and translated by G. A. Wenzel. Philadelphia, PA: Smith, 1881.

Williams, Delores S. *Sisters in the Wilderness: The Challenge of Womanist God-Talk*. Maryknoll, NY: Orbis, 1993.

Williams, Patricia A. *Doing without Adam and Eve: Sociobiology and Original Sin*. Theology and the Sciences. Minneapolis: Fortress, 2001.

Wink, Walter. *Engaging the Powers: Discerning and Resistance in a World of Domination*. Minneapolis: Fortress, 1992.

———. *The Powers That Be: Theology for a New Millennium*. New York: Doubleday, 1998.

———. *Unmasking the Powers: The Invisible Forces that Determine Human Existence*. Philadelphia: Fortress, 1986.

Yoder, John Howard. "Jesus and Power." In *On Earth Peace: Discussions on War/Peace Issues between Friends, Mennonites, Brethren, and European Churches, 1935–75*, edited by Donald F. Durnbaugh, 365–72. Elgin, IL: Brethren, 1978.

———. *The Politics of Jesus: Vicit Agnus Noster*. 2nd edition. Grand Rapids: Eerdmans, 1994.

—. *Preface to Theology: Christology and Theological Method.* Grand Rapids: Brazos, 2002.

—. *The Priestly Kingdom: Social Ethics as Gospel.* Notre Dame, IN: University of Notre Dame Press, 1984.

—. *The Royal Priesthood: Essays Ecclesiological and Ecumenical.* Edited by Michael G. Cartwright. Grand Rapids: Eerdmans, 1994.

25542408R00089

Made in the USA
Middletown, DE
03 November 2015